EMOTION

in

CHORAL
SINGING

Reading Between
the Notes

Is expressive singing—or expressive music-making in general—purely intuitive? What precipitates beautiful and communicative singing, and is it more than "we like the piece" or "I understand the text and have a story to tell"? While these questions are worthy to ponder, Jameson Marvin's *Emotion in Choral Singing: Reading Between the Notes* provides an insightful, brilliant, and logical discussion of the connection between notation and the singers' and audience's understanding and communication of the text and its musical garb. Practical and detailed in its chapters on process, lofty and big-picture in its sections on humanity's desire to express, *Emotion in Choral Singing* comes at choral singing from a musician's musician perspective. One immediately senses that Prof. Marvin speaks from both the podium and the scholar's desk with an authority that is genuine and helpful.

> Jerry Blackstone
> Professor Emeritus
> School of Music, Theatre & Dance
> University of Michigan, Ann Arbor, Michigan

Rich in historical context, this valuable book includes detailed discussions about the many aspects of score preparation, the rehearsal process and choosing worthy and appropriate repertoire. It also lays out in an insightful and comprehensive manner the numerous things a choral conductor must consider in order to bring to life the meaning behind the composer's musical symbols. A significant addition to the literature on choral performance.

> Joseph Flummerfelt
> Artistic Director Emeritus
> Westminster Choir College, Princeton, New Jersey

This book captures everything that Jim Marvin believes and has brought to students and colleagues through his music-making for many years. This volume is full of phrases like "the greater the degree of compositional integrity, the richer the rewards the singers experience," and "clarity of insight inspires conductors, inspirational conducting motivates singers and motivated singers inspire each other and the conductor." His ideas of tuning, text and its relationship to the other elements in the score, the conductor's process, programming, and rehearsing are insightful, practical, philosophical, and brilliant!

> Ann Howard Jones
> Professor Emerita, School of Music
> Boston University, Boston, Massachusetts

EMOTION
in
CHORAL
SINGING

Reading Between
the Notes

JAMESON MARVIN

Foreword by Simon Carrington

GIA Publications, Inc.
Chicago

G-9607

GIA Publications, Inc.
7404 S. Mason Ave. Chicago, IL 60638
www.giamusic.com

For recordings of 12 representative performances by Harvard University ensembles conducted by the author, including works analyzed in this book, visit giamusic.com/emotion

Cover and layout design by Martha Chlipala.
Edited by Kirin Nielsen.
Printed in the United States of America.

DEDICATION ❧

This book is dedicated to my esteemed teachers and mentors with my life-long gratitude for traveling with them over my 50-year choral life:

to George Houle—a brilliant teacher who inspired me with his insights and enthusiasm for the performing practices of early music, and from whom I was profoundly enriched by his knowledge that especially deepened my love for Renaissance choral performance

to Robert Shaw, for his uniquely meaningful rehearsal techniques and the quality of energy in pursuit of his goal to bring a score to inspired aural life, and his clarity of thought in establishing the foundation of choral ensemble music-making that has stayed with me throughout my conducting career

to Helmuth Rilling, for his penetrating insights into sacred masterworks, often those on biblical texts, especially Bach's, his mastery (and teaching) of choral-orchestral conducting, and his gift of confirming in me the importance of word/music relationships and how they are a catalyst for meaningful, expressive choral performance, offering a deep emotional connection

and to my student singers of Harvard University for giving me the opportunity to teach, rehearse, and conduct you, for 32 years reenergizing a community of kindred spirits, by working hard to give meaningful and communicative aural life to seven centuries of choral music we sang.

ACKNOWLEDGMENTS ∾

One of my goals in retirement from Harvard University was to write a book. Above all, I wanted to write a book based on the core values that I had acquired over fifty years of experience in rehearsing and conducting choirs.

At an ACDA conference I mentioned my idea of writing a book to Alec Harris, President of GIA Publications. Alec responded immediately to this idea and his reaction galvanized my efforts to begin to write. Alec, thank you very much for your continued support throughout my journey.

I am very grateful to Kirin Nielsen, Associate Editor of GIA Publications. Her superior knowledge of choral literature and choral topics have guided my book with authority and with deep editorial insight. Throughout the editorial progress of my book, Kirin's insight towards completion combined with teamwork throughout have meant a great deal to me.

Simon Carrington has written the Foreword to my book. I am profoundly grateful to Simon for his breadth of insight and erudite thoughts. His knowledge of our profession and esteemed musicianship offer my book a rich perspective. Simon and I have known each other for more than forty years. We share common philosophies and insights into the topics explored in my book and a kinship of spirit about choral music-making. I am so thankful for Simon's engaging thoughtfulness in writing the Foreword.

Emotion in Choral Singing: Reading Between the Notes is my first book. Given my predisposition for verbosity, I knew I would need considerable guidance and editing skill. I cannot imagine writing this book without the expertise, experience, and thoughtfulness of my friend Dr. David Wilson, Choral Professor Emeritus, University of Southern California. For more than a year and a half, David read each chapter with considerable grace, and ongoing wide-ranged editorial expertise.

I first met David at the University of Illinois. He and I were graduate students pursing DMA degrees in choral music during the late 1960s. We have enjoyed our friendship for over 50 years, and especially appreciate the musical perspectives and complementary choral expertise we share. Three years ago I realized that David was also an excellent writer. He asked me to read his new book on "The Dresden Manuscripts," and if I would mind writing a review of it for the ACDA *Choral Journal*; I was happy to do so. I mentioned to Dave that I too had been thinking of writing a book, and asked if he might be willing to read a chapter or two of some preliminary drafts I had made. He immediately responded that he would be happy to help.

I am deeply grateful to David Wilson for his thoughts, time, musicianship, and choral expertise in helping me to edit all sixteen chapters. As we emailed back and forth for nearly two years, David's edits became an integral part of my progress in helping me to bring to life the drafts of my book, in anticipation of submitting it to GIA for publication. His experience, wisdom, and insightful edits gave clarity, specificity and power to my thoughts. David's editorial expertise was offered to me with uncommon patience and generosity.

Polly Marvin, my wife, knows well my range of emotions concerning attainment of good rehearsals and performances. She is also quite familiar with my unharnessed verbosity in speaking and in writing. Polly is a master at expressing thoughts succinctly and she is also an experienced and excellent choral singer. She attended every concert I have conducted over the past 35 years, and has offered me continued support as I toiled away, trying to form a good sentence. In the past, Polly has helped edit my speeches, short articles, and lecture demonstrations. As an administrator in the healthcare profession for many years she has worked with physicians, peers, and patients in editing their writing to gain their desired communicative effect.

Polly has bettered the clarity and meaning of countless sentences throughout the many chapters of my book. Not only do I thank Polly for helping me with editorial suggestions, but for having unbelievable patience about the number of hours I spent in my home office, hooked to my computer.

Polly Marvin, I am grateful beyond words for your support and appreciation for what I have been trying to do for the past two years, for your understanding of my drive to pursue this goal, and for your endless love and ongoing support. The content of the book contains familiar knowledge which Polly had heard many times at home, and the *title* of the book is a marriage of both of our ideas.

TABLE OF CONTENTS ∾

PART II

PART III

APPENDICES

FOREWORD ∽

by *Simon Carrington*

I first read the manuscript of this wonderful book on a train to Birmingham (UK) on my way to a choir rehearsal. I was so excited and stimulated by what I was reading that, by the time I arrived that evening in the university choral room, I had changed my entire rehearsal plan and re-evaluated my approach to choir training! Jameson Marvin has filled this book with essential techniques, suggestions, and recommendations from the bottom of his warm heart. He provides an invaluable and inspired lexicon for all of us whose passion it is to gather individuals together, be they students, keen amateurs, or seasoned professionals, and to fashion them into a choral ensemble ready to share their love of music and words with those around them.

As I was reading, I remembered how I had invested in a small library of what were considered essential guides for the choral director when I began my teaching career. I dutifully assembled several worthy tomes on the shelves of my studio and eagerly prepared to use them as references for my graduate conducting students. I have to admit now that, after some initial probing, these books remained forever where they were, gathering dust. Had Jameson's book been available I would have been a happier man, as I would have found myself in the company of someone who feels deeply about the "expressive gestures hidden behind the notation," who champions so eloquently my own belief that polyphony is an essential ingredient in the recipes we use to encourage and train choirs small and large, and who emphasizes constantly that subtle dynamic nuance wedded with rubato is as important for choirs as it is for orchestras and instrumental chamber ensembles.

As I sat in that train I was constantly brought up short by the realization that I had forgotten this or that aspect of the rehearsal process, that I had been ignoring this or that key element in my score preparation, or that I had been overlooking the importance of this or that dissonance and had therefore discounted a vital tool in the composer's expressive vocabulary. We all need constant reminders to consider what nuances our choirs can apply to clarify the composer's thinking.

I have known the author ever since we met many years ago after a King's Singers concert in Boston Symphony Hall. We discovered then that we shared many of the same ideas about choirs and choral music and have remained firm friends. His book distills with engaging and infectious excitement the value and importance of the teaching of polyphony in all its forms and provides an important reminder to us all that "compositions of unrelieved homophony diminish the chance for students to take on the responsibility of crafting their own separate parts as polyphony shapes and challenges the musicianship of singers." He writes, "when rhythms and melodies are separated from one another, choral singers are freed from the relentless experience of harmonizing the principal melody" and again "maintaining and projecting expressive nuances in a contrapuntal fabric of multiple voices is challenging but stunningly rewarding." My lifetime of music making includes a quarter century of concerts around the world as co-founder and director of The King's Singers and a decade of symphony and chamber orchestra concerts with some of the world's great maestri during my double bass playing days, yet one of the memories that still moves me the most is of my University of Kansas chamber choir standing under the fourteenth-century spire of Salisbury Cathedral, singing Tallis's peerless forty-part polyphony in his motet "Spem in Alium."

During my first year conducting the choirs of The New England Conservatory in Boston I attended a performance of the Bach *St. Matthew Passion* conducted by Jameson at Harvard University which I have never forgotten. It wasn't just the matchless singing of William Hite's Evangelist and the other fine soloists, or the stylish playing of the period orchestra, or the accuracy of the articulation and the impeccable intonation, but rather the commitment and the dedication to the story-telling of the student chorus which made such an impression. No-one in the theatre that night could have doubted the belief stated so often in these pages that just reproducing harmonies, rhythms, melodies, and textures in performance may not necessarily mean the choir is singing music.

Jim Marvin encapsulates and expresses the key ingredients which distinguish choirs and choral ensembles that move us by the way they communicate to their listeners an understanding of the composer's intent. Quoting multiple sources, he ensures that we conductors base our interpretative decisions on sound scholarship and that we always remember that medieval chant (and chant-style singing) is one of the most important sources of expressivity in the performance not only of Renaissance polyphony but of all the choral music that follows. He includes valuable and detailed analyses of significant choral works from a range of styles and periods and leaves us in no doubt that giving the singers the responsibility of perceiving the relationship of text to music, of grading the internal balance, and judging the refinements of the tuning under the conductor's guidance are essential components of a unified musical concept.

His chapters are bursting with practical ideas, useful tips, multiple wise observations, and historical references to help us think again about what we do and how we do it. Jim Marvin's fifty years of undying enthusiasm, his effervescent personality, and self-effacing service to the composers he loves pervade these disarming paragraphs. They are permeated by his unflinching belief in the qualities that distinguish performances that "provide uplifting and enriching experiences and embody the ultimate goal of music—transcendence."

> —*Simon Carrington*
> Yale University Professor of Choral
> Conducting, Emeritus
> Visiting Professor of Conducting,
> University of Birmingham, UK

PREFACE ❧

EUPHORIA

In March of 2004, while on spring tour with the Harvard Glee Club, I had the occasion to sit next to a freshman singer. I have always enjoyed spring tours because they offer opportunities to get to know new students. During an engaging conversation, he asked me, "How did you get into choral conducting?"

I thought how shall I best answer this question. There are so many places to begin. So, I began at the beginning and told the young man that when I was a boy I loved to whistle! I was a good whistler. I whistled favorite tunes I heard my grandmother sing and play on the piano, especially Stephen Foster songs, folk songs, Americana, hymns, and Christmas carols. I loved whistling those tunes, and prided myself on my ability to whistle both blowing out and sucking in. That way I could keep a continuous seamless line with or without vibrato. One day, I decided I should take whistling lessons. I was aware of a peculiar effect that whistling had on me; I seemed to slip in and out of a sort of dream world as these melodies issued from my lips. I really liked the sensation.

I asked my mother, who had listened to my astonishing whistling feats from every room in the house, "Mom, can I take whistling lessons?" A big smile came across her face as she answered, "What a good idea, Jim. I know someone who just might give you lessons." "Great!" I blurted out, with my characteristic enthusiasm.

I told this new freshman, who by now was getting drowsy, that's how it began! Mom contacted Mrs. Olson, the mother of one of my elementary school friends. We went to her house, rang the doorbell, and Mrs. Olson invited us in. Mom explained that I wanted to take whistling lessons. Mrs. Olson smiled knowingly, took me over to her piano, sat me down, and said, "This is middle C."

Well, you can guess where this went. Mrs. Olson did not have a clue about how to whistle, but she turned out to be an excellent piano teacher. It was through playing piano and listening to my grandmother sing and play that I was drawn to music.

Unlike most children, I loved to practice. Every morning, I got up early, around 5 a.m., went downstairs, and began to play the piano. Over the years I developed a huge repertoire. I would sit and play to my heart's content. Why? It was the dream-like state I felt when I played that drew me in. Off to another world I would soar— *euphoria*. That was why I loved to play. In high school and in college I began to realize through performing or listening to music I could experience that ecstasy. While piano was my principal outlet, singing in choirs (junior high, high school, church, college, and graduate school) allowed me to experience that euphoric feeling I so loved.

Continuing my story to the slightly revived Glee Club freshman, I told him that at University of California at Santa Barbara, my undergraduate school, I joined a fraternity. Fraternities, sororities, and dorms competed in what was a marvelous tradition: Spring Sing! Besides first and second place in each division, the top award was

Sweepstakes. Since I was one of the few men in my fraternity who had a music background, I was asked to conduct. I loved it! I realized I enjoyed standing in front of a large group, waving my arms, leading them towards something I heard in my head, what I now call my "mental-aural image."

My experiences in conducting and singing led me in my sophomore year to switch my major to music. There was no conducting degree, so I majored in music theory, history, and composition. During the summers, I formed choirs to sing during services at my home church. At UCSB I sang for four years in the Men's Glee Club and Chamber Singers. Both were immensely rewarding. In my senior year, I conducted my fraternity, and we won Sweepstakes.

The repertoire of the Chamber Singers led me to Renaissance music. Singing the rich polyphonic sacred works of the Renaissance brought me again to that euphoric state I remembered so well. I began graduate studies at Stanford University where I received an enriching education in the performance practice of Renaissance, Baroque, and Classic music. For me the revelation was experienced through the masterful teaching of George Houle. At Stanford, I was also the assistant conductor of the Memorial Church Choir and majored in choral conducting with a specialty in Early Music Performance. My experiences at Stanford were enormously rewarding.

After completing my Master of Arts degree at Stanford in the summer of 1965, I was accepted to the new DMA Choral Program at the University of Illinois. The faculty included renowned choral directors, musicologists, theorists, and early music specialists. Harold Decker was the Chair of the Choral Division and became a wonderful mentor. He was a highly skilled conductor with a vast knowledge of choral literature spanning the fifteenth to the twentieth centuries.

The combination of my early experiences at Santa Barbara singing with and assisting the Glee Club and the Chamber Singers, the inspiring education I received at Stanford in the performance practice of Renaissance and Baroque music, and the deep grounding in choral literature at the University of Illinois formed an important foundation in pursuing my choral career.

By now, the Harvard freshman was asleep, but I rambled on.

My first job was a one-year sabbatical-leave position at Lehigh University, an all men's engineering school at that time with an outstanding Glee Club. My experience singing with the Glee Club at Santa Barbara was an invaluable preparation for the conducting position at Lehigh. Each year the Glee Club joined a number of women's choirs to perform major works. One of them was Vassar College, and during my year we combined to perform Bach's *Magnificat.* The Vassar College conductor, who appreciated my work with the Lehigh Glee Club, asked if I would conduct his choir while he was on sabbatical leave. When Vassar became a coed college, the music department asked me to form a new mixed choir and to continue to conduct the excellent 100-voice women's choir.

Nine years at Vassar led me to Harvard, primarily through my experience of working with men's and women's choirs, coupled with my knowledge of Renaissance choral performance, ten years of experience conducting major works, and my expertise in women's, men's, and mixed choral literature.

My thirty-two years at Harvard University as Director of Choral Activities and Senior Lecturer on Music was a life-changing experience, one that I loved, and one that fit well with my background, experience, musicianship, and personality. It is to these students who taught me, inspired me, and allowed me to develop *choral ensemble music making,* that I dedicate this book.

For over forty years there has been a constant: the search for *euphoria*. It is this experience I consistently want to share with my singers. The heart of this book therefore is concerned with emotions. Understanding the emotional content of notation and the symbolic representation of pitch and duration is the Leitmotif that permeates this book. Developing the insight and ability to lead choruses in rehearsals to experience this sublime state, the collective ecstasy of "euphoria," has been my goal.

I believe choral music has the power to draw us into a spiritual realm, a transcendence that allows a fleeting moment of peace. In today's world, and in fact throughout time we have sought feelings of transcendence. To be able to absorb and reflect upon humanity's greatest source of strength, the contemplation of an essence impossible to understand but made manifest by the incomprehensible mystery of life gives us strength, enriches our souls; and it reconfirms humanity's greatest gift: the capacity to love.

INTRODUCTION ∽

A s I approached retirement from Harvard University in 2010, I began to think about writing a book on my many fields of interest and expertise. My intention was to offer a new perspective for experienced choral professionals, teachers, advanced students, and conductors just entering the field. I believe what is often missing today in choral performance is the subject of this book: *the emotional connection.*

Musically, technically, and substantially, this book provides insights into six complementary fields:

1. Musical Gesture and Emotion: A Guide to Teaching and Performing
2. The Historical Roots of Singing: Notation and Expression
3. Performing Polyphony in the Twenty-first Century
4. Style and Expression in Renaissance Choral Performance
5. The Conductor's Process
6. Mastery of Choral Ensemble

Symbols, Gestures, Emotions

The historical *raison d'être* for singing is to express emotion. In *Music: Physician for Times to Come*, Don Campbell uniquely describes music as "an organization created to dictate feelings to the listener. The composer is an unrelenting dictator, and we choose to subject ourselves to him when we listen to his music. This means, of course, that there are two kinds of musical experiences: music being thought and organized—the world of the composer—and music listened to, subjecting oneself to another's musical thought. That the two worlds have something in common is testimony to the universal qualities of human experience . . . the most intimate is unmasked as the most universal."[1]

How can we recapture this intrinsic truth today when confronted with notational symbols written by composers from diverse historical eras representing individual languages of expression? What do symbols of pitch and duration actually mean? Does notation mask the intentions of the composer? What may the composer be trying to express that cannot be represented in the notation? Can our imaginations illuminate the unseen feelings within the notation? What keys help unlock the composer's emotional vocabulary? Campbell remarked, "Music of Beethoven, Mozart, and Bach is not just a remarkable organization of sounds ... it is capable of giving meaning to life, to place man in a hierarchy within which he can look up, and the energies associated with such a view."[2]

We know that singing flourished in the centuries long before signs of notation occurred; in fact, research reveals that the origins

---

1   Don Campbell, *Music: Physician for Times to Come* (Wheaton, IL: Quest Books, 2006), 125, 126

2   *ibid.*, 126

of singing began with the earliest *Homo* lineages. The consensus confirms that singing developed during the development of speech. Countless centuries later, symbols began to appear, written down by scribes as hints of the aural tradition of chant. The symbols were in essence mnemonic devices to remind singers of the melodies sung for over eight centuries

These first symbols looked like squiggles written above the sacred text to remind the singer of the melodic contour and how the melody was sung. While scholars do not know the precise meaning of all these signs, they do know they carry reminders of expressive nuances, such as dynamics, stresses, motion, and duration. As Richard Hudson writes in his insightful book, *Stolen Time: The History of Tempo Rubato,* "in the ninth century before the staff had been invented to identify pitches precisely, letters sometimes appeared above the *neumes* to indicate a special method of performance . . . the letter *c,* for example, refers to Latin words such as *cito* or *celeriter* which means 'rapid'; *t* to *trahere* or *tenere* means to 'drag out or hold'."[3] For eight centuries chant was an aural tradition. When notation began to appear in the ninth century, the purpose of the symbols placed above the words was to convey how the chant was sung, not to provide the notes and rhythms. The symbols became guidelines for expressivity.

By the thirteenth century, chant symbols evolved into neumatic notation with neumes written on a four-line staff. Neumes representing notes and rhythms were often connected in groups of two, three, four, or five notes. In the fourteenth century, more florid melodies ornamented the syllables or words. This style evolved into the early polyphonic motet. The motet became the foundation upon which Western choral music was based, flowering into the rich polyphonic

---

3   Richard Hudson, *Stolen Time: The History of Tempo Rubato,* (Oxford: Oxford University Press, 2004), 5

tradition of the Renaissance. The development of this flowering can be seen in the motet, mass, chanson, and lieder. Beginning with fifteenth-century master composers Dufay, Ockeghem, and Josquin, continuing with sixteenth-century successors Lassus, Palestrina, and Byrd, and culminating in the sacred genres, madrigals, and concerted works of Monteverdi and Schütz, polyphony flourished.

POLYPHONY

"Where Have All the Flowers Gone?" The question refers not only to the neglect of singing Renaissance music but also the neglect of the magnificent polyphony of the seventeenth through the twenty-first centuries. Performing polyphony seems rarely considered today.

To our traditional multi-voiced, multi-sized choirs directed by conductors in churches, schools, communities, and colleges, I ask, "how can we bring to life the profoundly enriching panoply of styles of the fifteenth through the early seventeenth centuries? How can we project the expressive power and beauty of Renaissance music so that it offers a wellspring of emotion to our singers and audiences?"

THE CONDUCTOR'S PROCESS AND MASTERY OF CHORAL ENSEMBLE

My essay titled "The Conductor's Process"[4] (chapter 2) seeks to make conscious what we do as choral conductors. In essence, it is an overview of our responsibilities, from choosing repertoire to training choirs for performance. "Mastery of Choral Ensemble"[5] (chapter 7) serves as a practical guide, offering valuable and specific advice about how to teach and rehearse choirs to sing at their highest level.

---

4   *Five Centuries of Choral Music*, ch. 1.

5   *Up Front!*, ch. 8

The underlying premise of both articles offers a complementary and comprehensive perspective on four major topics: 1) score study and the development of the mind's ear (our mental-aural image); 2) internalizing and reflecting our mental-aural image of the music to our choir as we seek to attain the eventual goal; 3) rehearsing: the core of the choral art; how we teach this fundamental process to the choir, and what methods can be taught in rehearsals to lead choirs towards achieving matching conceptualizations; and 4) preparing the score for listening and the ear for hearing—the conduit through which sound information passes in order to make the rehearsal process work.

PART I:
EMOTIONS AND SYMBOLS

CHAPTER 1
HISTORICAL SINGING ❧

INTRODUCTION

Throughout history, there can be little doubt about music's capacity to inspire, uplift, and rejuvenate spirits. Moments of mourning and rejoicing, past and present, have elicited group-song, joining the collective cathartic spirits and experiences of the participants. Anthropological research reveals that singing began with the *Homo* lineages countless centuries before notation developed. From the very earliest times to the present, group singing has been a response to feelings and emotion. Spontaneous singing initiated by internal emotions is inherently human.

Does notation distance us from expressing emotion, the *raison d'être* for singing? Do the notes as presented in score notation obscure meaning? Can symbols of pitch and time mask an understanding of the emotional content of compositions? What is going on between the symbols, among the notes? Might we be deeply curious about the inherent *meaning* of the notational symbols that beg answers to these questions? What is the composer trying to tell us? How do we express his or her emotional conception?

The development of Western notation coincides with the singing of chant. Chant melodies decorated the emotions of the text. The development of squiggles (mnemonic devices) written above the sacred words reminded singers of the melodic contour of the chant and *how* they were to be sung.

Today, symbols of pitch and time are accurate, but score reading itself can distance us from taking the initiative to look beyond the *explicit* information and how it may relate to the *implicit* meaning behind written symbols. Finding unseen expressive nuances the composer may have had in mind is the challenge. Once we understand the *implied* rhetoric (the inherent expressive vocabulary) of past centuries, we will acquire the insight and understanding of the composer, perhaps even imagining what emotion the composer felt.

ORIGINS: EXPRESSING EMOTIONS: NEANDERTHALS AND HOMO SAPIENS

Homo sapiens were not the first among our lineage to sing. In his illuminating book, *The Singing Neanderthals*[6], Steven Mithen explores the earliest connections between song and speech. His research offers insight into the origins of meaningful communication and the historical understanding of the interrelationship of song-speech in *Homo* species, especially Neanderthals and *Homo sapiens*. "Music invokes some of the same neural regions that language does, but far more than language, music taps into primitive brain structures involved with motivation, reward, and emotion."[7]

---

6   Steven Mithen, *The Singing Neanderthals: The Origins of Music, Language, Mind, and Body*, (Cambridge, MA: Harvard University Press, 2006).

7   Daniel J. Levitin, *This Is Your Brain on Music: The Science of a Human Obsession*, (New York: Plume/Penguin, 2007), 191

When we hear music, we experience moments of tension and release, anticipation and resolution, growth and decay, and sound and silence. These qualities create moods that signal change. Amplifying, complementing, and enhancing emotional consciousness through the diverse communicative mediums of pitch, duration, timbre, and intensity is music's inherent gift. Mithen's research describes the manner in which Neanderthals expressed diverse emotions and the how and why singing evolved as a method of expression of emotion in later *Homo sapiens*.

HOMO SAPIENS (WISE MAN)

Emotions and their expressions are at the very center of human life and thought. Mithen explains that there was a single precursor for music and language: "a communication system that had the characteristics of both music and language but that split into two systems at some date in our evolutionary history."[8] Anthropologists confirm that 20,000 years ago modern humans had developed language, cognitive fluidity, and music. Our ancestors' physiological development of neural circuitry enabled the *Homo sapiens* to separate music and language.

Language and music are combined when we sing. Composers write words under symbols. What do the symbols mean? Composers imagine "how the music should go." In choral music, the meaning of "how the music goes" is derived from the study of the symbols by the conductor. The conductor transmits his or her knowledge to the choir. Choirs sing, giving aural life to the notation. The composer's setting of the words gains emotional meaning.

The choir's challenge is to communicate. How? Through pitch, duration, timbre, and intensity, the catalysts for breathing the aural

---

8   Steven Mithen, *The Singing Neanderthals: The Origins of Music, Language, Mind, and Body*, (Cambridge, MA: Harvard University Press, 2006), 24.

meaning of a composer's mind's ear are transferred. Expressive nuances may be expressed by notation, yet hidden gestures behind the notation may reveal the composer's mind's ear, what he or she expects to hear. This book seeks to illuminate the composer's imagination and complete the circle, from language to music, composer to conductor, conductor to choir, and choir to the audience.

While today we know that language is best expressed through speech, and emotions are better expressed through music, the development of "proto-language" in Neanderthals and earlier *Homo* species offers a perspective on the historical evolution of group gatherings in which ideas and emotions were expressed and shared.

Words, emotions, song: that's our "proto-language." Rehearsing and performing choral music mirrors this deep link to our ancestry when we gather for group singing. Music becomes a medium through which individual brains are coupled in a shared activity of social bonding, creating an experience of common emotions that envelops, enriches, energizes, and develops a profound community of kindred spirits.

HISTORICAL NOTATION AND THE SINGING OF CHANT

Thomas Kelly, my colleague at Harvard University, provides penetrating research on many historical genres and composers. Over his career his insights into medieval music and chant performance are fascinating and informative. Two of his most recent books are relevant to choral directors: *Early Music: A Very Short Introduction*[9], and his richly detailed and beautifully illustrated book, *Capturing*

---

9   Thomas Forrest Kelly, *Early Music, A Very Short Introduction* (Oxford: Oxford University Press, 2014).

Music: The Story of Notation[10], relates the development of chant notation from the last years of the eighth century up to the beginning of the fourteenth century.

Christian chant has existed since the beginning of the Church. We know little about the history of chant until chant manuscripts first appeared in the early ninth century. Research reveals that the manner in which chant was performed changed considerably over the centuries. The notation of chant varied greatly, and over time changes in scribal practices and notational systems increased.

Early medieval notation revealed many characteristics. As Kelly states, "This is a notation that tells *how to sing* the song, not what the song is; but it does not tell us what the notes are or how long each one is."[11] Chant notation appeared in varied combinations of vertical, horizontal, and slanting *squiggles* of many sizes placed above the words. The squiggles not only reminded singers of the melodies but also *how to perform* the melodies.

As Richard Hudson points out in his fascinating book, *Stolen Time: The History of Tempo Rubato*[12], "it [chant singing] is concerned with the proper accentuation of words and syllables, the rhythmic shaping of phrases, sentences, and other structural units, and the projection, on a very subtle level, of the meaning of the text."[13] Writers in the tenth century refer to "tempo change at cadences, a gradual ritard, slowing for phrases at important structural tones, lengthening the last two notes."[14]

---

10   Thomas Forrest Kelly, *Capturing Music, The Story of Notation*, (New York: W. W. Norton, 2015).

11   Kelly, *ibid., 54*

12   Hudson, *Stolen Time*, 4–5

13   Hudson, 5

14   Hudson, 5

As notation developed, the complexity of writing offered details that go beyond the notes and contain many expressive nuances. Today, musicologists and medievalists understand many of the *expressive meanings* of the squiggles. As Kelly points out, many of these relate to "voice quality, ornamentation, rhythmic articulation, and melodic direction."[15] In referring to *tempo,* tenth century writers noted many chant performance phenomena from slowing at the end of phrases and especially lengthening the last two notes. Hudson comments, "In addition, the shapes of the notes could indicate tempo changing. A ritard or lengthening of a note is shown by enlarging a portion of the neume figure, by separating notes that would otherwise have been joined together, or by adding a horizontal stroke."[16]

These varied notations and the evolving practices of singing were meant for monks in churches and monasteries who sang chant every day throughout their lifetime. Today we realize by reading reports from monks and theorists that experienced singers could make sense of this notation only if they had a good memory. Kelly comments, "The notation works perfectly, assuming you already *know* the Song! Only an experienced singer with a good memory can make any use of it. Perhaps the chief reason for writing music neumes was not to record the melodies themselves, but *how you perform* those melodies."[17]

Early notation does not tell us exactly what the notes are because the notational symbols were not designed for that purpose. As Kelly summarizes, "it's not just a question of the notes: it's a question of the *music,* and this notation, like many other early forms, has a remarkable elegance and finesse; it ought to give us a sense of what early medieval chant sounded like." Scholars understand these symbols as relating to

---

15   Kelly, *ibid,* 54

16   Hudson, *Stolen Time,* 5

17   Kelly, *Capturing Music,* 54.

expression. In this way, the words below (in italics), taken from the varied descriptions of chant nuances described by Kelly and Hudson, show how they may relate to today's terminology.

Today's terms	Terms scholars use to describe expression in singing chant
Dynamics	*emphasis; volume, light, fleeting, weight*
Phrasing	*smooth, connected, separate, lengthened, shortened*
Articulation	*articulated, light, heavy, separate*
Linear Direction	*fluid, connected, fleeing, ritarded, phrased, separated*
Rubato	*hasten, motion, fleeing, ritarded, lengthen, hold*
Singing	*connected, separated, tremulous, ornamented, articulated*
Sound	*at final syllables, vowels, consonants,* and *diphthongs, color* [18]

In the year 1030 at the Cathedral of Arezzo, a monk named Guido who trained singers for the cathedral described a new system of notation that transformed the art of singing. As Kelly confirms, it was "one of the simplest but most radical technological breakthroughs in the history of writing music."[19] Guido invented a revolutionary system: a four-line, pitch-specific musical staff.

As staff notation developed, *neumes* (notes) appeared in varied forms on the staff, from single neumes to neumes visually connected in groups of two, three, four, or five, either ascending or descending. The connections represented *symmetric* (two note) and *asymmetric*

---

18   Kelly, Ibid, 55, "the change in the shape of the mouth, a description of the closing down of the vowel sound".

19   14 Kelly, *Capturing Music*, 62.

(three note) *micro* phrases. Shifts of emphasis (groupings) in patterns of twos and threes allowed for subtle expressive nuances in singing chant. Chant-style singing is one of the most important sources of expressivity in the performance of Renaissance polyphony.[20]

While the notational staff and the information it offered is salient to an understanding of a composer's craftsmanship, the emotion a composer wants to express is not clear in staff notation. As Barthold Kuijken states in his book *The Notation is Not the Music: Reflections on Early Music Practice and Performance,* in chant notation we see the notes and rhythms but we don't know the emotional rhetoric that accompanies the score. The title of Kuijken's book reveals a profound thought: *this concept can be applied to all scores.*

Expressive nuances are rarely notated in music prior to the 1650s.[21] By the late seventeenth century markings began to include other word modifications such as *ritardando* and *rallentando*. By the middle of the eighteenth century many descriptions of expressive nuances— especially mood modifiers of tempo as well as phrasing, articulation, and dynamic markings—became more prevalent. Increasingly, scores appeared with more explicit expressive marks which communicated ideas of how the composer felt her composition should be performed.

However, if we follow only these explicit markings we miss the boat. We must uncover the *implicit* (emotional) gestures implied by the notation itself. In order to clarify the elusive nature of unwritten implicit feelings, conductors must first understand the text/music relationships revealed through the composer's compositional craftsmanship. In analyzing the composer's notational vocabulary,

---

20 See Chapter 15, Performing Renaissance Choral Music

21 In Heinrich Schütz's *Geistliche Chor-Musik* of 1648 there is one motet, "Ich weiss, dass mein Erlöser lebt," that contains one word, "tarde," an expressive tempo indication meaning "slower."

structure, style, and the composer's musical imagination, including "what happens between the notes," conductors can glean the emotional language of the composer's musical intent—her mind's ear.

Informed study uncovers the mental-aural image of the composer's conception. This conception is transmitted to the choir. It is in the rehearsal that the conductor teaches the composer's conception to the choir. The rehearsal prepares the choir to perform compositions with conceptual clarity and insightful expressivity. From choosing the repertoire, to studying and teaching it, then presenting it at the final concert, these components comprise the multi-faceted art of The Conductor's Process, which is the subject of the next chapter.

CHAPTER 2
THE CONDUCTOR'S PROCESS[22] ⌒

INTRODUCTION

The purpose of this chapter is to provide a *conscious* perspective of the multi-faceted concerns of the choral conductor. The interrelationship of each element within the Conductor's Process is illustrated by the diagram of the process on the following page. At the center of the process is *rehearsing*. While each aspect of the conductor's process has an impact on at least one other, and the composite of the whole represents the ideal conductor, each of the elements cannot be fully realized without the ability to rehearse.

The *performance* (8) is the ultimate motivating goal for the rehearsal, but it is not the goal of the process. Before the performance, (7) *rehearsing* takes place; and before the rehearsal, (1) *literature must be chosen*, the (2) *score studied*, and questions concerning (3) *style and performance practices* need to be addressed. Through

---

22   The Conductor's Process" is an article I wrote for *Five Centuries of Choral Music: Essays in Honor of Howard Swan,* edited by Gordon Paine, Stuyvesant, NY: Pendragon Press, 1988.

stylistic and structural analysis, the conductor develops a (4) *mental-aural image* that prepares the conductor for (5) *rehearsing*. In the process of rehearsing, the conductor uses his (6) *ear*, (7) *conducting technique* and (8) *rehearsal acumen* to lead the choir toward a unified musical concept of the composition.

Specific skills needed in the preparation of the rehearsal are: *piano* proficiency, *language* skills (translation and pronunciation), *vocal* training, and for concerted works, a knowledge of orchestral *instruments*. The complete conductor aspires to excel in all these aspects. It is a life-long process.

The arrows in the following diagram illustrate the relationship of the elements of the conductor's process. The direction of the arrows signifies either a one-way or a circular connection. The most complex relationship is between the *mental-aural image,* the *ear,* and *rehearsing*. It is through the ear that the conductor measures his mental-aural image against what the choir is singing. Having an indelible image of the musical concept of the score acts as a powerful stimulus in directing the choir toward that image. The degree of technical, musical, and conceptual mastery of the score by the choir is therefore dependent upon the conductor's aptitude and abilities in rehearsing. The ear provides the information necessary to make the process work. Each element of the process requires a lifetime of study and demands continuous attention. The complete process, by nature, is self-perpetuating and nourishes (9) *communication, inspiration,* and *rejuvenation*, the life-blood of the profound interaction between humanity and music.

The principal objective in discussing each aspect is to make explicit common assumptions and to provide a more conscious perspective on the art in which choral conductors are engaged.

Figure 1. *The Conductor's Process*

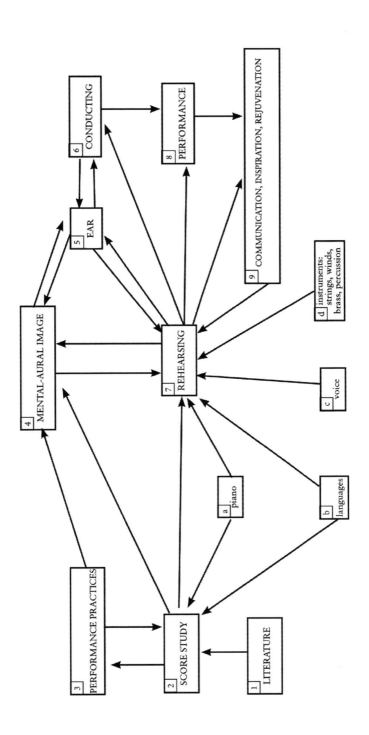

A Career of an Inspired Conductor: An Interview with Robert Ward[23]

RJW: In your essay you state, "The performance is the ultimate motivating goal for the rehearsal, but it is not the goal of the process." What is the goal of the process?

JNM: The *process itself* is the goal. The process is the time I spend with the students and the music. We work as a team. The hard work, the fun, and the laughter are part of the process of exploring the *meaning* of the composer's vocabulary and discovering what is expressive in the music. Of course, the students look forward to the concert, especially when it involves a major work, but the concert is a one-time event. It's the process of perfecting the music that the students find so rewarding. That's what counts, that's education, and that's inspirational.

RJW: When you work with choirs, you are very particular as to the exact place and space for each singer. What are your views on the placement of singers within a given acoustical space?

JNM: Fundamental to a productive rehearsal, the singers must be able to *hear* the entire ensemble as well as hear themselves and ideally not be influenced by a singer on their own part. I frequently rehearse and perform in quartets. Placing singers in quartets functions as an encouragement to both the ensemble and the individual singer. At the same time, it is important to have space between the singers, as much as one full arm length. We rehearse in a horseshoe position that mirrors a C, so the ends can hear each other. This forms an acoustical "cup" that allows singers to create an acoustical space. Singers must be able to hear the ensemble. If they cannot hear problems, they cannot fix them.

---

23   Robert Ward, Professor of Choral Music, Ohio State University, entitled the article, "A Career of an Inspired Conductor" that was published in the ACDA *Choral Journal*, May 2007, 16–23. It is based on an interview Dr. Ward had with JM at Harvard University.

RJW: Should the conductor stand outside of the horseshoe or deep within? Where is the best position for the conductor to hear?

JNM: I hear best somewhat within the horseshoe. This means students on the very ends of each row might momentarily see my back. I am basically in front of the group and frequently turn from side to side to include all singers.

RJW: Singers in your choirs tell me that you place tremendous responsibility on each singer to achieve their own level of intonation, so that it is not just the conductor assessing intonation, it is also the singer that assesses their own intonation. Is that accurate?

JNM: Yes, you are correct, but first I have to teach them what it is to be in tune. Often choral singers have little experience with what singing in tune means. We start by listening for overtones: the octave, 5th, and 3rd. I play a low note on the piano for them to hear the 5th, the 3rd and the octave produced by the low note. Often I ask the basses to sing a *unison* low A (or G), and students are then asked to listen for the octave, 5th, and 3rd they produce. I find cupping the ears helps the process. It becomes clear that the 5th and especially the 3rd are not the same as the piano pitch.[24] We also discuss vertical (chord-tone) balance, timbre, and vowel unity. Over time, students learn to hear this, having established what "in tune" means (which usually takes two or three months). At the final cadence of a piece, I say "tune it"! Immediately the singers listen and adjust. I ask them, "can you hear the difference?" They always yes! I then ask them, "What did you do to make it in tune?" Using this procedure places the responsibility on the singers to remember what they *individually* did to tune the chord. I constantly teach them how balance, intonation, and vowels are interconnected.

---

24   The 5th is minutely low to the overtone; the 3rd is grotesquely sharp to the overtone.
     See Chapters 10, 11, and 15

RJW: So you are constantly challenging the singers to hear things better and to tell you what they hear.

JNM: Yes, it's an ever-present circle. While veterans help new members, once I know they all can do it, another world is open to them. Now when I say "tune it!" they *know* what to do. They do not do it automatically; I have to constantly remind the "big Harvard brains." The challenge is to capture those "big brains," but once their energy is focused, they can do anything I ask. It is quite amazing, but it's important to remember that singing in tune is not the end; it's a means to the end. I want them to sing in tune, in balance, with matched vowels, so the choir not only hears musical clarity, but is drawn into its beauty. That is the sound we seek also to draw in our audiences.

CHAPTER 3
CHORAL LITERATURE ❧

THE FIRST STAGE OF THE CONDUCTOR'S PROCESS[25]

Choral repertoire is by far the richest and most diverse of all musical forms. Conductors can select from the inexhaustible treasure-trove of music from the fifteenth to the twenty-first centuries. The major forms—Mass, motet, cantata, oratorio, Passion, Magnificat, Requiem, chorale, anthem, chanson, Lied, madrigal, folk song, and spiritual—are readily available in anthologies, collections, and collected works in college and university music libraries. Many publishers make available an enormous quantity of significant choral literature. Others cater to popular demand and are under financial pressure to publish music that is accessible but may not be of lasting merit.

The central thesis of this brief discussion is: *perform music of good quality.* Music of distinction performed well is an experience of significant value. In contrast, performing trendy easy-access music is by nature an ephemeral pleasure, a temporary titillation. Satisfaction

---

25 Throughout this book, especially in Part II, the stages of the Conductor's Process as well as Mastery of Choral Ensemble are explored more deeply.

of this kind of music is often short lived. Though the emotions it taps may be strong, this music rarely has the capacity to continuously enrich. Performing the treasure-trove of folk and indigenous music is important for gaining insight into the aesthetics and values of many cultures and countries. I love folk songs and have made many arrangements of wonderful songs for my choirs to sing on our tours around the world.

One of the profound rewards of performing choral music drawn from the vast heritage of seven centuries is the cumulative experience provided by insights into the cultural and aesthetic values of historical eras. Singers are challenged and invigorated by performing great works of choral literature. They acquire a broad perspective of aesthetic values. They learn the excellence of music and how it enriches their lives.

Great choral singing demands full participation in the process of creating, recreating, and listening. The rewards gained in performing great music—a Josquin motet, a Poulenc chanson, a Brahms motet, or a Monteverdi madrigal, and the masterworks: Stravinsky's *Symphony of Psalms*, Mozart's *Requiem*, Bach's *St. Matthew Passion*—are directly proportional to the mental and emotional energy put into rehearsing. The greater the degree of compositional integrity, the richer the rewards singers experience in meeting the challenge. By singing quality music, singers will experience the profound rewards of "enlightened cherishing."[26] To deny students the pleasure and life-enriching experience of rehearsing and performing repertory of the masters, obfuscates the conductor's principal purpose and primary responsibilities: educating and inspiring singers.

---

26   Harry Broudy, *Enlightened Cherishing: An Essay on Aesthetic Education* (Urbana, University of Illinois Press, 1971).

Choosing and Programming Repertoire[27]

Recently a student asked, "what factors go into your choice of repertoire and programming; what is your thumbprint or trademark of programming?" I responded with the following thoughts. First, I examine a lot of a cappella literature that choral ensembles will learn each year in preparation for their spring tours. I also think about what combined choral-orchestral works the choirs will perform each year. My choices for both categories depend on time management, scheduling, and offering for students a diversity of repertoire over a four-year period.

The process of determining repertoire takes much time mostly during the summer. As I play through innumerable compositions I try to determine which pieces are worthy of rehearsing and performing by asking myself, "Is it a work worth trying to perfect? Will it capture the singers' enthusiasm? What is the composition's degree of difficulty? How long will it take to master it? How and when can I program this piece?"

I estimate about one hour of rehearsal equals one minute of music, depending upon degree of difficulty and number of vocal parts. Specific repertoire choices relate to concert timelines. One principle I consistently hold is not to care how long a concert will last, but to care about the time it will take to learn the repertoire.

I've learned good music sung well builds considerable ensemble pride. For touring repertoire, I choose a wide variety of genres: sacred, secular, a cappella, and accompanied. I gravitate toward sacred Renaissance repertoire; contemporary American, French, and British choral works; beautiful folk song arrangements; and the music of Brahms.

---

27 Excerpts from an interview through email correspondence with a graduate student at the University of Michigan, 2001–2002.

My "trademark" is to program uninterrupted sets of pieces (often three). I believe applause after each piece interrupts the singers' mood. A continuous exchange of energy between the choir and audience creates a confluence of evolving emotions. Normally, I do not program according to intellectual themes. I tend to link compositions that share structural and emotional qualities, such as linking a Renaissance polyphonic motet with a contemporary polyphonic sacred work. I link by musical texture and structure, and by contrast and complement. I find these criteria provide a wide spectrum of possibilities.

Ideally, the tonality of a piece relates to the next piece for easy transitions. I love to end a piece in a certain mood, then more to the next piece, which initially continues that mood, but by the middle it will have imperceptibly traveled to another emotion. The same connection and change occurs in the third piece, so that by the end of the set the conveyed emotion has changed again. Linking moods that complement, contrast, and change, over time creates ebbs of emotion. In that manner, I try to engage the audience by taking them on an emotional ride.

STANDARDS[28]

In April 1992, for the Repertoire and Standards Committee of ACDA, I submitted a repertoire list of about 250 works performed over the past fifteen years by the Harvard Glee Club[29]. It is gratifying to know this annotated list was helpful to many conductors. In that this list relates to the area of repertoire, I thought it worthwhile to write my thoughts about standards.

---

28 From an article published by the ACDA Eastern Division Male Chorus Repertoire and Standards Committee: *Troubadour,* April 1994, 6–7.

29 The complete HGC repertoire list, 1978–2010, appears in Appendix B.

"Standards"[30] —what a snobby word! I wish it were not part of the title of the committee for which I am Eastern Division Chair. But since it *is,* perhaps we should think about what "standards" means. According to ACDA committee structure, standards basically means two things: 1) standards of repertoire, and 2) standards of performance.

Ideally, the two definitions of standards can go hand in hand if the word "good" is included. Our goal is to perform *good* music *well.* But what *is* good music? Good music digs deep. If performed well, it is an experience of lasting significance. Good music performed well lives in our memories, even for a lifetime. Music of distinction has the power to inspire and enriches the lives of the participants.

As conductor of the Harvard Glee Club, I came to realize male chorus music is divided principally into these eras: fifteenth, sixteenth, and early seventeenth centuries, and nineteenth, twentieth and early twenty-first centuries. It is vast and highly differentiated, but compared to the inexhaustible treasure trove for mixed choir, the amount and quality of male chorus music is staggeringly small.

"Standards" may *sound* snobby, but standards are crucial to our lives, our profession, and our music making. Standards in choral literature must be paired with standards in performance. While disagreement concerning details of interpretation and opinions about choral tone are as common as conductors are different, few musicians and knowledgeable listeners fail to recognize an outstanding performance of excellent repertoire when they hear one. Such a performance of quality repertoire is an enduring experience, one that occupies a permanent place in our hearts. And best of all, rehearsing and performing great music well inspires us, makes us want to do it over again, and motivates us to tackle the next great piece.

---

30   Fortunately, ACDA recently has changed the title to "Repertoire and Resources."

In the male chorus arena, we should add one other standard that must be achieved: *the sound.* True, our literature is comparatively limited. The intrinsic nature of the male-chorus texture offers a limited range for composers. But the *sound*—now that is a highly motivating factor! Unifying the sound is the most rewarding aspect of male choral singing. If sung in tune with balanced vocal parts and matched vowels, an A major chord (A–E–A–C♯), is a transcendent sound, almost like an organ. Sound is the common love of the male-chorus singer. When we add the enriching reward of fellowship, the picture is complete. The more clearly we understand how this multi-faceted standard enriches our lives, the more meaningful the whole process becomes, and the more inspired we are to continuously pursue high standards.

To Publishers, Composers, and Conductors: Choosing Repertoire[31]

"Why do I want to perform *your* composition? Why do I want to publish *your* composition? Why do I want my choir to perform *your* edition?" The answers to these questions clarify our circular relationship.

We are all interconnected. Before I begin, it would be helpful to offer some thoughts about what I think the conductor's point of view is within this circle. Much of what I am going to say you already know or intuitively feel, but I thought it might be important to bring to the forefront the process conductors use in making decisions about whether or not to perform a specific composition, or choose a specific edition or publication of it.

---

31   In the spring of 2004, the Radcliffe Choral Society sponsored a Festival of Womens' Choirs. They invited twelve choruses as well as conductors, composers, and publishers of women's choral music. Below is a brief speech that I gave at our opening ceremony to addressed to composers, publishers, and conductors that describes our interconnections.

Personally, I am as interested in performing a motet by Josquin as I am in performing a Haydn mass, a Bach cantata, or Tarik O'Regan's latest composition. For example, this year the Glee Club is singing *The Four Prayers of St. Francis of Assisi* by Poulenc and a beautiful Sanctus from Tallis's *Mass for Four Voices.* The Collegium is performing the great motet "Warum ist das Licht gegeben" by Brahms and Frank Martin's *Mass for Double Chorus,* a twentieth century a cappella masterpiece.

This afternoon the Radcliffe Choral Society will perform a Sanctus from a Palestrina mass, a colorful secular piece by Veljo Tormis, a moving and compelling composition by Hilary Tann, and an incredible folk song arrangement by me! So, I'm stimulated by a wide variety of compositional styles and genres and by many works written by composers today. I especially enjoy looking at publications of a cappella gems for mixed, men's, and women's choruses. I'm thrilled to stumble upon a choral/orchestral masterwork from the seventeenth, eighteenth, nineteenth, or twentieth centuries. These gems and major works seem to be the apples of my eye. There are lots of apples! I consistently want to perform these apples, in fact, I can't wait to bite into them.

Why? Why do so many works seem to charge me up? Why do I want to perform *your* music? It begins, of course, with score study; that's when I really get fired up. Why do I get fired up? Because I think it is a good piece, I like the piece, I like the text; it speaks to me. I know the choir will like the piece; they will have enough time to learn it, and I can't wait to teach it. Compositions I choose offer educational benefits or some insight into values: cultural, aesthetic, historical, stylistic, philosophical, spiritual, emotional, and musical.

How do I make this decision? There are many overlapping answers, but I think for me it is trying to figure out how the music is related to the text. I try to understand why the composer wrote what she or he wrote. When I look at a score in any depth, I am intrigued by the hidden gestures implied by its symbolic notation. I find this search often leads to answering the question why do I want to perform this piece. It is because I have come to understand the answer to the "other question": why the composer wrote what she or he wrote.

It is this revelation that I find incredibly compelling: because I want to share it, and I want to tell my students about it. As I sit at the piano, I imagine myself doing just that. In rehearsals when I say to the singers, "the composer didn't *have* to do that," and we discover together "why" he or she *did* that, their excitement is palpable, their enthusiasm grows, they understand; they get it!

This thought is powerful. The real answer to the *why* question, the catalyst for why I choose a piece of music, is found by experiencing an emotional connection to the composer's composition. The connection may be immediate or may take place over time, but it is the emotion that I feel for a piece of music that motivates me to teach and conduct it. These insights are the catalysts that can draw students closer to experiencing the magic moments of inspiration fired by the transcendent power of music. For conductors, these thoughts and experiences answer the questions: "what inspired the composer to write what she/he wrote?" and "why do I want to perform the composition?"

CHAPTER 4
SCORE STUDY ❧

PHILOSOPHY[32]

The second stage of the Conductor's Process is the foundation on which choral performance is based: score study. In acquiring thorough knowledge of the score, the conductor prepares for the rehearsal and develops the perspective and security upon which to base the composer's vision.

While music notation conveys an enormous amount of information, realizing the notation in sound requires conceptualization of all the information that the symbols imply. Bringing the score to aural life requires imagination. Score conceptualization is the catalyst that fires the imagination. Imagination inspires the conductor's mental-aural image of the music and creates the *mind's ear*. The conductor's *mind's ear* becomes a powerful energizer in motivating singers to achieve a unified aural vision of the composer's intentions. Although the score represents pitch and time, and, depending upon

---

32   Throughout this book, especially in Part II, the stages of the Conductor's Process as well as Mastery of Choral Ensemble are explored more deeply.

the era, includes expressive marks, the composer's imagination may not be completely transmitted. *Notation is not the music!*

A clear expression of this concept is written by Daniel J. Levitin in his book *This Is Your Brain on Music.* In Chapter 7, "What Makes a Musician," he writes, "I am not a [Frank] Sinatra fanatic . . . but on *Songs for Swinging Lovers* every note he sings is perfectly placed in time and pitch. I don't mean 'perfectly' in the strict, as-notated sense; his rhythms and timing are completely wrong in terms of how the music is written on paper, but they are perfect for expressing emotions that go beyond description."[33]

The challenge is to lift the music off the page and bring it to life by creatively employing the expressive elements: tempo, dynamics, phrasing, articulation, energized linear direction, and rubato, with clarity of tuning, balance, matched vowels, and meaningful dissonances. Bringing to aural life this composite picture sets in motion the Conductor's Process.

The core of score study is structural analysis: the study of the relationship of the total design of the music to the details that order its architecture. Harmony, melody, rhythm, and texture form the building blocks of structure. Duration, pitch, timbre, and intensity articulate the sound-continuum of the form and design. All these elements interact with text. The degree to which text inspires or affects the elements of music is an important question to be addressed.

Throughout the history of western music, *words* have inspired the masterpieces of choral literature. Words impose order and prescribe limits. Furthermore, there is an inherent dialectical tension between words and music.

---

28   Daniel J. Levitin, *This Is Your Brain on Music,* (New York: Plume/Penguin, 2007), 193.

No other controversy in music history better illustrates this tension than the polarity of positions held by musicians at the dawn of the Baroque who espoused the principles of the *prima prattica* and those who championed *seconda prattica*. The two conflicting philosophies are best summarized in the preface to Claudio Monteverdi's *Scherzi musicali* of 1607, written by his brother, Giulio Cesare. *Prima prattica* is described as a technique of composition which is "not commanded [by the word], but commanding; not the servant, but the mistress of the word. *Seconda prattica* is "not commanding [by the word], but commanded and makes the words the mistress of the harmony."[34]

Discovering which of these aesthetic principles governs the composer's creation deserves considerable thought. In the hands of one composer text may serve as a vehicle for displaying compositional craftsmanship. In another, words may be the catalyst that generates the structural and expressive elements of the composition. Once the kernel of inspiration is perceived, the text/music relationship understood, and the form and structure analyzed, the conductor gains insight into "the truth" of the composition, the ultimate goal of score study.

---

29   Oliver Strunk, trans., *Source Readings in Music History,* rev. ed., Princeton University Press, 1965, 535–544

CHAPTER 5
PERFORMANCE PRACTICE ∿

Overview

Since the 1960s there has been an enormous surge of interest in the performance practices of prior ages. Theoretical treatises, performing manuals, and modern scholarly investigations form the collective body of knowledge from which performers try to glean information about the performing practices of former eras. The third stage of the Conductor's Process examines the principal concerns of performance practice research: tempo, phrasing, articulation, pitch, temperament, tuning, dynamics, rubato, instrumentation, timbre, ornamentation, improvisation, *musica ficta*, basso-continuo realization, and the size and make-up of performing forces create windows of opportunity to gain insight into the varied performance practices of previous eras.

There is great value in attempting to understand the expressive nuances inherent in the ways our forebears made music. The philosophy that encourages performers to learn about the performing practices of prior eras does so with the expectation that the more we detect about what a composer wanted and expected to hear, the more likely we will be able to create an intrinsically expressive performance.

Understanding style and transmitting its meaning to students and listeners requires educating (and re-educating) our ears. Furthermore, over the centuries, notation has changed considerably. Today's musical symbols convey specific meanings, but their contemporary meaning is not relevant to the performance of yesterday's music. Because the meaning of many symbols has changed over the centuries, the original intent may be lost, or blurred. Written symbols of sound from any era (often misinterpreted the further we go back) ultimately can never completely convey what a composer had in his mind's ear. It is up to us to "fill in" what was most likely intended.

The process of discovering meaning in music of the past and gaining insight into the intrinsic expressive values of prior eras is invigorating. The rewards are particularly rich when singers and audience begin to open their ears and minds more sensitively (and pleasurably) to the art of appreciating the performing styles of earlier music.

Research and score study yield a wealth of information and insight; it offers a window into the past, yet there are still uncertainties. No one living has heard Bach perform one of his cantatas, and no one knows how each of Handel's Foundling Hospital performances of *Messiah actually* sounded. We have little idea of how the singers of the Sistine Chapel performed Palestrina's Masses. Nor do we know enough about how Mendelssohn and Brahms performed tempo relationships in their multi-sectional motets.

It is sometimes possible to take the "purist approach" too far. Worse, is to allow authenticity (even knowledgeably imagined) to be the end in itself. Some musicians, lacking in imagination with a predisposition toward scholarship, offer dull, lifeless performances in the name of authenticity. Insightful, imaginative performances, grounded in stylistic understanding of inherent expressive nuances, are not synonymous with perfunctory performance. Intelligent, informed music making that provides uplifting and enriching experiences embodies the ultimate goal of music—transcendence. Without the soul of the music, merely answering authenticity questions in performance has little value.

Ideally, conductors strive for a balance. But at the heart of the philosophy underlying the concern with performance practices, basing modern performance upon aesthetic values of past eras, invites conflict. The conflict centers on value systems—those of past eras and those of our own. Education, taste, and personal preference all play a significant role in choosing which value system forms the foundation upon which performance rests.

If Bach had our performing forces—that is, more singers and the modern orchestra—what would he have done? In the context discussed, this is an outdated question. The question is more sophisticated: which insights and informed priorities shall we choose from the performing and aesthetic principles of the past to make our performances meaningful today?

Serious conductors ponder this question each time they prepare a new score. Answers vary greatly if we are to judge by the standards of today's recorded performances of music of past eras. However, choosing the most pertinent expressive values of former eras and combining them with our own in a fresh, new, communicative spirit, will enliven and deepen the performance experience.

HISTORICAL PERFORMANCE TODAY

In contrast to our common listening experiences, it is interesting to note that at the court of Mantua in 1592 the new sound of the dominant 7th, beginning especially in Book IV of Monteverdi's madrigals, would have startled the court audience with its audacious, harsh, and seemingly unnatural sound.[35] In early fourteenth century cathedrals, the harmonic sound of the major 3rd, most pleasing and pleasant to us, was experienced as dissonant.

Among many viewpoints, we share a commonality of modern tastes. Why should we not perform choral music today for our audiences, who have twenty-first century ears? In this context, one might ponder if Palestrina had the resources of the 250-voice Mormon Tabernacle Choir would he have wanted it?

In considering this question, Palestrina wrote for his choir at the Cappella Giulia, the Papal Chapel in Rome, named for Pope Julian II. Payroll records tell us that between 1571 and 1594, Palestrina had between 18 to 24 singers in the Cappella Giulia, the principal musical establishment of St. Peter's. It is also probable that the Pope, with the wealth of Rome, could afford to hire the largest choir in all of Italy. The Pope's choir of 18 to 24 singers was considered uncommonly large[36] the average church choir being only 8 to 12 singers.

Composers were singers and leaders of their choirs; they wrote for their own choir. The sound in their ears was the sound of their choir or of a neighboring cathedral or a court that might perform the composer's music. He wrote music based on the compositional principles of his teachers, historical theorists, private instruction, and

---

35 No better examples occur than in Books IV and V, published at the turn of the seventeenth century, that mirror the *Seconda Prattica*, stressing the emotion of the words over the strict polyphonic texture.

36 For festive occasions such as weddings, special feasts of the church year, and memorial services, the Choir might employ up to 40 singers.

the study of past composers. The composer assumed, and certainly expected, that his music would sound a certain way, for it is likely the composer conducted it.

In that light, some of us may have the wrong sound in our heads. To allow Renaissance music to speak to audiences today, it is invaluable to educate ourselves in the aesthetic values common to the fifteenth and sixteenth century.

With more than 40 years of experience in conducting Renaissance repertoire with choirs that have consistently numbered between 50 to 70 singers of mostly non-music majors, I found that the two most important elements to maintain in performing music from 1450–1650 are: 1) clarity of intonation, balance, vocal timbre, ensemble rhythm, and 2) fully engaging in the expressive elements by which Renaissance choirs shaped musical meaning: tempo, tuning, dynamics, phrasing, articulation, linear direction, and rubato.[37] Choir size relates entirely to achieving clarity of vocal parts, well-balanced polyphonic lines, vocal timbres well-matched, and consistent attention to ensemble rhythm to achieve clear vertical alignment in polyphonic textures. Today, many choral directors strive to achieve these goals in performance. Renaissance music deserves this same attention! I confirm that large choirs *can* perform choral music of the Renaissance exceedingly well.

OTHER THOUGHTS ON INTERPRETATION

I generally approach a score intuitively, analyzing the harmony, melody, rhythm, texture, and how these elements shape the form and structure of a composition. I seek to discover the expressive gestures implicit in (though hidden behind) the notational symbols

---

37   See Chapter 13 "Performing Renaissance Choral Music"

of the composer. In that context, I also ask myself, "what should happen *between* the notes?" In this stimulating process, I develop my "mind's ear." I verify my conceptualization by continually trying to understand "how this piece ought to go." The results of in-depth study develops consistently in me a very strong mental-aural image: "*this* is how it goes!"

In making aesthetic decisions concerning performance practices of past eras, I choose eternal musical attributes as well as those stylistically inherent to the composition when it was composed. It is important to make decisions about what was important then and what is not important now. What *is* important now is the way I juxtapose old and new aesthetic values. For me, the primary focus (ensemble rhythm, intonation, balance, matched vowels) is achieved in rehearsal. These technical elements form the foundation upon which I place the gestural elements that illuminate the intrinsic style and expression in performing Renaissance music.

CHAPTER 6
CONDUCTING[38] ⟨⟩

PRECISION AND CLARITY

From the *tactus leader* of the Renaissance, the keyboardist of the Baroque, and the first violinist of the Classical era, conductors have traditionally been an integral part of their music-making ensemble, a singer or an instrumentalist who also "kept time." Until music achieved the complexity of a work like Beethoven's *"Eroica" Symphony*, the principal function that conductors served was to provide pulse; they marked time and kept the ensemble together. Conducting as a separate profession is a comparatively recent phenomenon.

Today's conductors no longer just keep time. They seek to represent sound-images that take place in time. Their conducting technique is expected to reveal musical meaning as well as pulse and meter. The foundation of modern conducting technique, therefore, rests principally in two areas: (1) representing clear information about pulse and meter, and (2) differentiating and highlighting musical events.

---

38   The completed discussion of the Conductor's Process occurs in Part II: The Core.

Visual representation of metric organization is historically rooted in very natural principles: (a) the *down* motion indicates the principal beat of the measure, which coincides with the pull of gravity; (b) the *up* motion, which is against the pull of gravity, is felt to be comparatively unstable, requiring resolution, the inevitable preparation for the *down*.

There is something about verbalizing arm motions that rivets my attention to "naturalness," the idea that gravity (felt unconsciously) harnesses physical arm motions to convey emotional energy clarifying pulse, tempo, metric organization, and musical gesture by visually representing: 1) resolution, strength, prime; 2) tension, unstable, stress; 3) contrast, differentiating, secondary; 4) weakness, nearly inconsequential.

EXPRESSIVITY: HIGHLIGHTING MUSICAL NUANCES

The modern conductor is expected to do more than clarify pulse and meter. She is expected to elicit expressiveness, to draw out musical gestures through physical gestures. Mirroring musical nuances through illustrative conducting gestures visually supports the structure of the music as it moves through time. In that light, conductors employ expressive gestures to visually amplify sound-images, moment by moment. Expressive conducting serves the music and allows performers informed access to its meaning.

Expressive conducting tries to convey musical gesture through the physical representation of it. To the degree that a conductor follows this principle, she will physically maximize important gestures and minimize unimportant ones. She will differentiate, and in this way, highlight musical meaning.

At the most expressive levels of communication, however, this process may impinge upon the projection of information regarding pulse and meter. Deciding which is the most important function—to serve expressive needs, or to project pulse and meter at any given moment—is a principal concern in the art of conducting. With experience, gifted conductors instinctively achieve an appropriate balance.

Grounding one's conducting technique in the principles of revealing pulse, meter, and the expressive elements of music, arms the conductor with a repertoire of physical gestures that will be universally understood, and serves the creative process of music making. As the conductor's technique becomes second nature, concentration increases. In rehearsal, a conductor will be able to more effectively implement change, and in performance she will be able to simultaneously respond to technical or musical concerns, providing confidence and security for the performers.

How odd it is that the act of waving one's arms has anything to do with the realization of sound! Why should physical gesture have an impact on performers?

The answer lies in the art itself. Physical gestures require energy and generate energy. The quality of the response is a mirror of the quality of the energy projected. The more meaningful the conducting gesture, the more focused the energy. The more focused the energy, the greater the power to elicit the desired response. Onward flows the circle of energy from conductor to chorus and back to conductor. The cycle is revitalizing for both. This process is real but invisible, often felt to be spiritual, and its essence inspires and enriches the lives of the participants.

PART II:
THE CORE

CHAPTER 7
MASTERY OF CHORAL ENSEMBLE³⁹ ∾

INTRODUCTION

A profoundly inspired choral performance provides singers and audience with deep fulfillment and lasting memories. When a conductor produces such a performance, a number of provocative questions may emerge. Why does the choir sound so beautiful? What is it that moves me? What is so compelling and inspiring about the choir's performance? How were the structural components of the composition revealed so clearly that the performance elicited the feeling that the audience was hearing the music for the first time? How did the choir achieve such a high level of mastery?

This chapter provides insight into the process conductors use to achieve the highest levels of choral performance. Mastering the choral ensemble—a unified sound image of the whole—is the foundation upon which enlightened, communicative, and inspiring performances

---

39   "Mastery of Choral Ensemble" is an article I wrote for the book, *Up Front!: Becoming the Complete Choral Conductor;* ed. Guy B. Webb, Boston: E. C. Schirmer, 1994.

take place. It is the goal toward which conductors aspire. The scope of knowledge, musicianship, experience and personal talent required to achieve an inspired level of choral mastery is limited only by the preparation and ability of both the choir and conductor. Ultimately, it is a humbling experience to meet the challenges necessary to perform good music well.

In rehearsals, conductors ask choral singers to bring aural meaning to a set of notational symbols through the mediums of time and pitch. This process requires thinking. It also requires clear insights to a number of questions: Why did the composer choose this text? How does he aurally illustrate the text through the visual symbols of pitch and time? What were the composer's expectations of the conductor? What would be the interpretive ideas that would bring to life the composer's expectations? Would a conductor see a composer's expressive vocabulary *implied* by the notation? Before rehearsals, conductors must think about the priorities they choose upon which to base their conceptualization of the score. The conceptualization will form the conductor's *mental-aural image,* a vision of what the music should sound like. It is the "mind's ear."

The foundation for developing this mental-aural image is achieved through score study, style analysis, and discovering the composer's expressive vocabulary. Fired by imagination, the mental-aural image becomes a powerful motivating agent. In each rehearsal, it provides the conductor with an ever-present standard against which to measure the choir's progress. The conduit through which the conductor measures the choir's mental-aural image is her ear. The process conductors use to instill their mental-aural image of the score into the "mind's ear" of the singers is *rehearsing.*

Over time in rehearsals the choir begins to mirror the conductor's conception of the score. The core of the process that conductors use in rehearsal is *teaching*: teaching each singer how to be responsible for providing and maintaining a meaningful, communicative sound-image. Ultimately, the responsibility for projecting this unified sound-picture resets with the singers. In rehearsals the choir learns to consistently reflect and project a unity of ensemble and mastery occurs, inspiring the singers, the conductor, and the audience. Inspiration rejuvenates participants and activates the compelling desire to "do it again." Through this profoundly creative process, choirs and conductors are drawn together to experience the continuing transcendent power of choral music.

CHAPTER 8
SCORE STUDY: DEVELOPING THE MENTAL-AURAL IMAGE[40] ~

By analyzing the form and structure of the score and resolving questions concerning stylistic priorities, the conductor conceptualizes his interpretive ideas, the mental-aural image. This image is an aural vision of what the music should sound like, the mind's ear. As the conductor carefully studies the composer's notation, his insights expand to develop a consciousness of the expressive gestures hidden behind the notation. This knowledge represents the *composer's* mind's ear. We try to imagine what the composer heard when he composed the piece. The deeper the insights into the score, the clearer the mental-aural image becomes. Clarity of insight inspires conductors to attain their vision. Inspired conductors motivate singers. Motivated singers inspire each other and the conductor. The process is self-renewing.

---

40   From "Mastery of Choral Ensemble," pp. 100–101

AN APPROACH TO SCORE ANALYSIS

Conductors develop insights into a composition by determining the composer's intentions, how the text relates to musical structure, harmony, melody, rhythm, and texture. As a conductor's insights deepen, information is internalized, and the result creates a conductor's mental-aural image. The thoughts below offer specific suggestions for conductors to develop a clear mental-aural image of a composition through analysis.

1. Text considerations
    - the relationship of text to the overall form of the composition and the text relationship to the primary structure that provides coherence to the form
    - the influence of text on the principal cadences which define the structure within the large form
    - the influence of text on sub-structures, the smaller cadential points
    - the relationship of text to each musical element: harmony, melody, rhythm, texture, instrumentation
    - The relationship of the text to each element of the *implied* expressive nuances
    - the influence of text on modes and keys: major, minor, modal
    - the influence of text on chromaticism, dissonance, harmonic progression(s), chord choices, chord juxtapositions and modulations
    - the relationship of text on melodic shapes, contours, and intervals
    - the influence of text on the tessitura and range of the vocal parts

- the influence of text on melodic lines and motives
- the relationship of text to meter
- the relationship of text to rhythms
- the influence of text on note combinations (long, short, symmetric, asymmetric)
- the influence of text on how note-groupings that provide syllabic stress may be contrary to the meter
- the influence of text on tempo

2. Texture considerations
   - how high, low, open, closed, dense, opaque textures may reflect the text
   - how the number of parts and the changes in texture may be influenced by the text
   - how texture, polyphonic, homophonic, linear, or chordal – may relate to text

3. Instrumentation considerations
   - how text influences the composer's choices of instruments
   - how text may relate to changes in orchestration
   - how text may relate to contrasting or complementing instrumental colors
   - how instrumentation gives greater meaning or depth to the text

4. Performance practice, style, and interpretive considerations
   - tempo, tempo fluctuations; tempo markings; mensuration; proportion; meter
   - phrasing (long note-groups; short note-groups); linear direction; syllabic stress
   - Gregorian chant asymmetric phrasing (groupings of "3s and 2s")

- Articulation, clarity of fast notes and emphasis of strong/ weak syllabification
- pitch level, temperament, tuning
- dynamics and rubato
- musica ficta
- basso-continuo realization
- cadential ornamentation
- balance, size, make-up of performing forces

SCORE MARKING[41]

Marking the score, like taking notes, reinforces learning. The process forces conductors to see details, and provides visual reminders of his mental-aural image. Marking the score insures that the conductor internalizes his conceptualization and prepares his ear for listening.

The mental-aural image, developed through analyzing the relationship of the text to the form, harmony, melody, rhythm, texture, expressive marks, and instrumentation, provides the foundation for rehearsing. By marking the score this sound image becomes deeply etched in the conductor's mind. It is important to remember that the score contains only written symbols of pitch and time. Conductors must discover the meaning behind the symbols.

Acute hearing is best developed by concentrating on the four basic elements of music: *duration, pitch, timbre, and intensity.* The conductor's interpretive ideas are linked to one or more of these four elements. The expressive elements of music are highlighted by: *dynamics, phrasing, articulation, linear direction, and rubato* written or implied by the notation. The following outline integrates score analysis by overlapping expressive components with each element of

---

41   From "Mastery of Choral Ensemble" in *Up Front!: Becoming the Complete Choral Conductor.*

music including their internal ingredients.

1. Duration: balance, dynamics, phrasing, articulation, rubato, linear direction
    *   pulse (tempo)
    *   rhythms; rhythmic groupings
    *   meter; mensuration
    *   macro and micro levels of the beat
    *   harmonic rhythm

2. Pitch: duration, dynamics, articulation, phrasing
    *   intonation
    *   quality, color, timbre
    *   intensity

3. Timbre: pitch, duration
    *   vocal sound–color–sonority
    *   vowels, pitched consonants: *m, n, l, v, z, ng, rr*
    *   resonance

4. Intensity: duration, pitch, timbre
    *   dynamics: structural, expressive
    *   articulation: syllabic accentuation or emphasis, consonants, clarity of quick passage-work, articulations of silence
    *   phrasing and linear direction: short note groups, short phrases; long note groups, long line
    *   rubato: shifts of intensity in relation to changes of duration; cadential influence; harmonic/melodic/rhythmic interaction; ritards, accelerandos

When the form, structure, text-music relationships, and interpretive nuances become clear, the composer's conception is revealed, especially when reminded by score markings highlighting the conductor's mental-aural image. In essence, a conductor re-edits the score to clarify the composer's mind's ear. A deeply etched clarity of the conductor's mind's ear is the foundation for the "re-edition," by writing in appropriate dynamics, phrasing, articulation, linear direction, rubato, concerns of balance, intonation, ensemble rhythm, and rhythmic independence.

Finally, compositional changes are an important element to mark in the score. Change reveals detail. Look for change in all elements of music: harmony, melody, rhythm, texture; pitch, duration, timbre, intensity; dynamics, phrasing, articulation, rubato, and linear direction; text mood relationships; and instrumentation.

The *core* of the conductor's process is the aptitude of the conductor's *ear* to measure the choir's sound against his mental-aural image. Chapter 9 illuminates the complexity of the conductor's process, with suggestions "how to hear," "how to listen," and "how to *fix*."

CHAPTER 9
PREPARING THE EAR AND THE SCORE
FOR REHEARSING ～

The ultimate goal, achieving *ensemble unity,* is the *core* of the conductor's process: studying the score and developing the mental-aural image; comparing the mental-aural image to the sound of the choir by *listening*; leading the choir to matching conceptualizations of the conductor's mind's ear through rehearsing (*re-hearing*). Effective rehearsing necessitates having a good ear, an indelible sound-image, refined rehearsal techniques, aided by score markings. Before beginning the rehearsal process, an understanding of the interlocking relationship of the four elements of music is important.

Each element—duration, pitch, timbre, and intensity—interacts and affects at least one other element. Pitch is perceived through duration, and its quality is identified by timbre. Intensity is felt through the interaction of pitch and duration. Duration provides the medium through which all three elements are given order and sound. Thus, the element of music that plays the greatest role in creating ensemble unity is duration. Expressive components of music (dynamics, phrasing, articulation, rubato, linear direction, and text syllabic nuance) are integrally connected with one or more of the four basic elements. These core elements are in turn influenced by nuances inherent in the performing practices of the entire corpus of choral literature.

Duration: Definition and Overview

Duration is defined by pulse, rhythm, and meter and makes possible the expressive components. When the primary objective of choral singing is directed toward *unity of duration*, pitch, timbre, and intensity can be more fully realized.

Unity of duration is achieved by establishing ensemble rhythm. Ensemble rhythm is the interaction of pulse on the rhythmic-metric-textural fabric of the composition. Training a choir to sing with good rhythm requires sensitizing choral singers to a unanimous group pulse. Individual internal "clocks" must perceive sound by the same scale of measure. By sensitizing physiological responses to the same scale, singers internalize pulse. As group pulse internalizes, ensemble rhythm develops. When ensemble rhythm is established, expressive components—dynamics, phrasing, articulation, rubato, and linear direction—are realized through duration, and will have an opportunity to project their communicative potential while singing.

Duration: Specific Principles and Tendencies in Rehearsing

The ability to hear notes that are moving fast or slow, or are short or long, is made possible through achieving clarity of diverse structural components. The following principles allow choral singers to hear many structural components comprising "duration."

FAST AND SLOW NOTES

Long held notes obscure quick moving notes. Decide what note value is the most important to be heard. Quick-moving notes generally serve expressive purposes; long held notes often serve a pedal or filler function, often at cadences.

Sing quick-moving notes with defined dynamics and clear articulation. Sing stationary notes that do not serve an expressive function more quietly or with a diminuendo to clarify structural balance.

Long notes can create dissonances that serve expressive functions or signal the approach of a cadence. When a held note creates a dissonance, highlight it just before the dissonance occurs with a modest quick crescendo that intersects the moving note with a quick stress-emphasis to "rub" against the long note.[42]

When long notes and short notes occur in polyphonic textures, points of imitation are structurally important and need to be heard. Highlight them with dynamic shaping, phrasing, and articulation based on the range, tessitura, and melodic relationship to the text.

In Renaissance polyphony, clarify micro-rhythmic note-groups of two and three notes; in later eras in Renaissance style, note groups are mirrored in imitative counterpoint.

In larger phrase structures that are derived from varied sources, clarify their aural meaning. These include:

- a composer's phrase marks
- the strong-weak syllabification of texts
- a conductor's wishes to highlight large phrases by connecting shorter (micro) groups;

---

42   In this context, humorously I refer to the *moving short note* as the *dissonator* that rubs against the *long held note*, the *dissonatee*.

- the mensuration and proportion signs in Renaissance music[43]
- hemiola phrasing which occurs at cadences in triple meters in much music of the fifteenth–nineteenth centuries.

TEMPO (PULSE): PRINCIPLES AND TENDENCIES

Choirs typically drag the tempo during the note-learning stage. Singers wait to hear the note before singing it. While a conductor at this initial stage needs to be flexible, it is important to keep the tempo goal in mind by consciously comparing one's internal clock to the choir's tempo.

Notes of consecutive equal value tend to rush. The accumulative *energy* when singing notes of consecutive equal value inevitably produces *rushing*. Listen for this natural ensemble phenomenon and draw the singers' attention to this problem.

Rethink tempi that in rehearsal seem too fast or too slow for the chorus or for the acoustics. Be aware of the strong impact consonants have on controlling tempo and on clarifying textures.

- In contrapuntal textures, especially with points of imitation sing relatively strong initial consonants with momentary stress to clarify entrances.
- Consonant placement requires time. Decide if a consonant occurs on the beat or before; pitched consonants (*m, n, ng, l, v, z, th,* and *rr*) require time to be heard and are placed before the beat.
- Orchestral instruments cover consonants. Exaggerate singers' diction when performing choral-orchestral works.

---

43 See Chapter 13

THE RELATIONSHIP OF TEMPO AND RHYTHM TO DYNAMICS AND PHRASING

Clarify phrasing with articulation to reveal long-note and short-note melodic groups. Employ subtle dynamics and rubato in melodic lines to highlight varied rhythmic passages, including: 1) changes of direction in each vocal line; 2) asymmetric micro note-groups derived in style from Renaissance polyphony; and 3) at cadences, to highlight the small or large structures that create the form.

In figure 1, these *very* momentary silences (indicated by commas) reveal the phrasing of nine varied note-groups in triple meters; gestural nuances are made apparent with momentary silences combined with adjustments of stress marks and phrase marks. With these markings a conductor can teach choirs musical nuances of notes in triple meter. In polyphonic textures contrasting asymmetric 3-note groups with symmetric two-note groups is made clear by these markings. Clarify the strong/weak syllabification of words by employing these note-groupings:

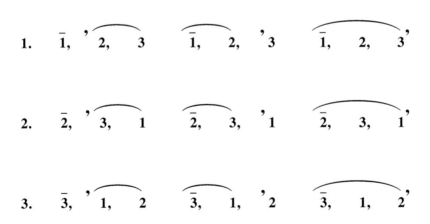

Figure 9.1. *Note groupings in triple meters*

In rehearsals, consider adding dynamics to note values to clarify structure. Have the choir sing whole notes *p*, half notes *mp*, quarter notes *mf*, eighth notes *f*. This will vividly reveal to singers the compositional structure, especially in polyphonic textures. Eventually modify these dynamics to allow the structure to sound more natural.

A hemiola prepares performers and listeners for the cadence; it beautifies and enhances the preparation by placing stresses on a rhythmic shift, revealing more clearly the gesture of *arsis* (preparation) and *thesis* (resolve). At the cadence, strength is the *arsis* and *thesis* is relaxation. In this way, crescendo and diminuendo are automatically implied.

Tempo shifts include ritards, accelerandos, and rubato. Conductors can initiate tempo change on any number of beats. Each choice will create a particular mood, emotion, or expectation. Tempo modifications are often simultaneously accompanied by dynamic change. *Rubato* seems rarely heard in choral performance today; it is an inherently expressive nuance that can accompany dynamics, phrasing, and linear direction. Make use of momentary silence; in essence allow a *very* brief *Luftpause*:

- at cadences between vowels and final consonants; for example: tou-| ch
- to highlight note-groups; as in figure 9.1 above: 1 2' 3 1' 2 3 1'
- to clarify textures and cadences at the completion of (long) held notes.

VARIABLE TEMPO RELATIONSHIPS

Tempo is a function of the following:

1. speed of harmonic rhythm,
2. clarity or opaqueness of the texture,
3. meter signature, and

4. composers' markings (*allegro, adagio, andante, largo*, etc.),
   Italian terms that describe mood more than a precise tempo.

RENAISSANCE TEMPOS

The natural speed of the *tactus* (pulse) was related to the *semibreve* (whole note) at about 60 beats per minute. Modern editions normally halve the composer's original notation; most Renaissance scores appear with the pulse related to the half-note.

The meaning of the term *alla breve* changes between 1400–1600.[44] The *alla breve* sign ¢ meant that the speed of the *semi-breve* (the whole note) is equal to the speed of the *breve* (two whole notes). From about 1400–1440 this theory remained, especially in conservative forms like the Mass, *chanson*, and *Lied*.

From c. 1440–c. 1525 the meaning of *alla breve* became modified to mean "speed up some," and by 1600 the *alla breve* sign became nearly irrelevant; the *alla breve* ¢ sign had lost its meaning, and ¢ and C became interchangeable because the notation had changed. The note values of the early Renaissance: longa, breve, whole notes, half notes, and quarter notes became smaller, commonly including eighth-, sixteenth-, even thirty-second notes.

TEMPO TRANSITIONS: HUMANISM, SECONDA PRATICA, AND THE BAROQUE

Changes in note values reflected the influence of *humanism*—the development of the compositional style of the latter half of the sixteenth century. Hints of this new direction are seen in the late motets of Josquin, and his successors, especially in the madrigals of Cipriano de Rore, Giaches de Wert, and particularly Claudio

---

44   See a fuller explanation in chapter 13, Performing Renaissance Choral Music

Monteverdi. By the late sixteenth century the motet and especially the madrigal became the vocal genres for composers to creatively highlight the emotional content of words. This became the driving force of the *seconda pratica.*

As the madrigal developed in the late sixteenth century, the emotional and sometimes literal suggestions of the text were mirrored in numerous ways in score notation. Eventually performers applied expressive elements not included in the notation, such as dynamics, rubato, and tempo change. Richard Hudson wrote, "Performers are described as singing fast and slow, as well as soft and loud, in response to the emotion in the text and music." [45]

In tempos of the seventeenth and eighteenth centuries, *tempo giusto* referred to the *just* or precise time. Frequently, the larger the meter (e.g., 3/2), the slower the tempo; the smaller the meter (e.g., 3/8), the faster the tempo. The use of an Italian word—a mood modifier placed above the meter—indicates the emotional nuance intended by the composer, most often related to tempo.

Bach and Handel frequently employ *stile antico* notation (*alla breve* signs with long notes to signify the old style). *Stile antico* strongly implied a pulse of two whole notes per bar, as in the second *Kyrie* of Bach's *Mass in B Minor.* It can be helpful to secure the vertical alignment by conducting in 4, emphasizing beats 1 and 3. Similarly, in contrapuntal textures of the sacred works of Haydn, Mozart, and Beethoven, the *alla breve* sign means two musical pulses per bar, though the vertical alignment of the counterpoint is made more secure conducting in 4, de-emphasizing beats 2 and 4.

---

45   Richard Hudson, *Stolen Time: The History of Tempo Rubato;* Oxford University Press, Clarendon Paperbacks, p. 6

TUNING THE CHOIR

PHILOSOPHY

Unifying pitch and singing with good intonation is one of the most elusive challenges in the choral art. When a choir sings in tune, the listener hears more clearly the music's structural components: harmony, melody, rhythm, and texture. Singing in tune heightens the awareness of structure that facilitates communication, and is more pleasing to the ear.

Good choral intonation is also beautiful. The sound of a choir singing in tune is an extraordinarily compelling experience. Good intonation reinforces the overtone series[46] and creates a rich sonority that invites the listener into the music and heightens the audience's awareness of the choir's beautiful sound.

Many factors affect good pitch: acoustics, environment, weather, health, the structural components of a composition, and most importantly, ear/voice coordination. All healthy voices housed in healthy energetic bodies have the great capacity to sing in tune. However, pitch and timbre together define intonation; a choir will not truly sing in tune until its composite vocal sound achieves a unity of timbre. The vowels as well as the pitch must be tuned. When vowels are matched, pitch can be unified, assuring that all voices sing with like frequencies and compatible timbres.

Singing in tune requires good ears, both the conductor's and singers', and requires consistent reinforcement. The responsibility for maintaining good pitch lies ultimately with the singers. While the conductor can initially provide a pitch standard, acquiring good pitch perception also requires an understanding of the process by

---

46   See Chapters 10, 11, 13, and 14 for detailed information

which it is attained. By teaching choral singers to become conscious of the process they use in attaining the conductor's pitch standard, the responsibility is then squarely placed on their shoulders.

The underlying philosophy answering the question "how do I get my choir to sing in tune?" is this: the conductor must teach singers how to teach themselves to sing in tune. Once this process becomes clear, choral singers are invigorated by the process. When the singers' choral intonation becomes good, ask them to remember how they "made it good." When the choir arrives at another chord that is well in tune, while they hold the chord, say, "tune it." Consider this idea frequently. Over time they are stimulated by their personal abilities to sing in tune.

TEACHING CHOIRS TO SING IN TUNE: INTERCONNECTED SUBJECTS AND MULTIPLE APPROACHES

Historical eras over the past eight centuries varied tuning systems that allowed certain intervallic relationships to be in tune with the overtone series: Pythagorean Tuning, Just Intonation, Mean-tone Tuning, and Well-Tempered Tuning.[47] The division of the octave into twelve equal parts is called *Equal Temperament*—the system by which pianos have been tuned for most of the twentieth century— and the system by which today's musicians including choral singers tend to measure pitch accuracy. Playing a composition on F♯ major would sound the same as on G major, other than it has a lower pitch. Most pianos are tuned to A-440 (440 beats per second). Most choirs sing written compositions of the composer in the written pitch. If the piece is without accompaniment, it can be transposed down or up a half (or whole) step.

---

47   See Ross W. Duffin, *How Equal Temperament Ruined Harmony (and Why You Should Care)*, W. W. Norton & Co. 2007.

USING TUNING SYSTEMS TO IMPROVE CHORAL INTONATION

There is no perfect tuning system. In all tuning systems there are *commas* (also called *flaws)* that represent the degrees of impurity imposed by tuning pure intervals. Tuning systems originated by developing acoustically pure intervals to sing (or play) music. In equal temperament, the imperfections (*commas* or *flaws)* appear in each half and whole step interval of an octave, both ascending and descending.

The Greek philosopher/mathematician Pythagoras (6th century BC) developed the first tuning system based on pure 5ths: C–G–D–A–E–B–F♯–C♯/D♭–A♭–E♭–B♭–F–C (which we now call the "circle of 5ths"); the final C is higher than the original C. In tuning pure 5ths: C–G–D–A–E, the resultant pitch "E" compared to the pure overtone E generated by the root "C" is irreconcilable. It is harshly dissonant, at least a quarter-tone *comma* out of tune. It is a *flaw* that is very easily heard.

By the fifteenth century, Just Intonation or Mean-tone Tuning of pure 3rds was developed. Pure 3rds were typically accomplished by tuning narrow 5ths: D–A–E–B–F♯–C♯ –G♯/(A♭) –E♭–B♭–F–C–G–D, producing pure intervallic 3rds: D–F♯ A–C♯ E–G♯ E♭–G B♭–D F–A C–E. The *comma* or *"wolf"* 5th at G♯–E♭ is very wide. This fact is important in realizing the innate out-of-tune-ness of equal temperament, and is mirrored by choral tendencies: descending half and whole steps will be slightly flat, and ascending half and whole steps will not be wide enough. Over time these intervals accumulate pitch problems, and the choir goes flat.

Attaining Good Intonation with Vertical (Harmonic) Intervals

Unisons, octaves, perfect 5ths, and major 3rds are the building blocks for tuning cadences or chords. Tune fifths very slightly high to the piano, and major 3rds low to the piano. Tune principal cadences to the overtone series;[48] sensitize singers to the overtone series in rehearsals.[49]

1. Major 7ths and minor 2nds cause pitch problems. Sing m2nds slightly wide and M7ths slightly narrow to piano pitch; clarity will emerge as the "smudged factor" of non-unisons and octaves will disappear.

2. Identify and clarify notes that cause dissonances in dense textures.

3. In "patches" of unexpected harmonies, search for "homing pigeon chords"—chords that are easy for singers to hear and to sing accurately. In a series of difficult intervals, these chords stick in the memory of singers and build a framework for aural security.

5. Ask singers to mark their scores with reminders of sharps, flats, naturals, wrong notes.

6. Practice listening to overtones. Pure overtone 5ths are slightly higher and Major 3rds are considerably lower to tempered piano tuning.

7. Tune principal cadences to the overtone series: 8ves = 2:1; 5ths = 3:2; 3rds = 5:4

8. Sensitize singers to these intervals. Teach singers to teach themselves to adjust to their own pitch at cadences.

---

48   See the discussion below about the acquisition of accurate tuning of perfect 5ths and M 3rds that match overtones produced by the root note.

49   See Chapter 14, Singing Polyphony Today.

9. Sing vertical minor 2nds slightly wide to piano temperament, major 7ths slightly narrower; 2nds become clear as non-unisons; 7ths become clear non-octaves.

10. In minor chords, sing vertical minor 3rds very slightly wider to piano tuning.

ATTAINING GOOD INTONATION WITH MELODIC (HORIZONTAL) INTERVALS

Sing *descending* half and whole steps and major and minor 3rds narrower; sing ascending half and whole steps and major and minor 3rds wider.

Ascending and descending intervals of 4ths, 5ths, 6ths, 7ths will require quick ear/voice coordination; bass root-position chords IV–I, V–I, VIII–I require careful pitch attention with accurate ear/voice coordination.

Below is a chart of 22 melodic formulas that invite flat pitch. The x marks the flat note; the * indicates the resulting flat pitch.

Figure 9.2. *Flatting tendencies in melodic formulas*

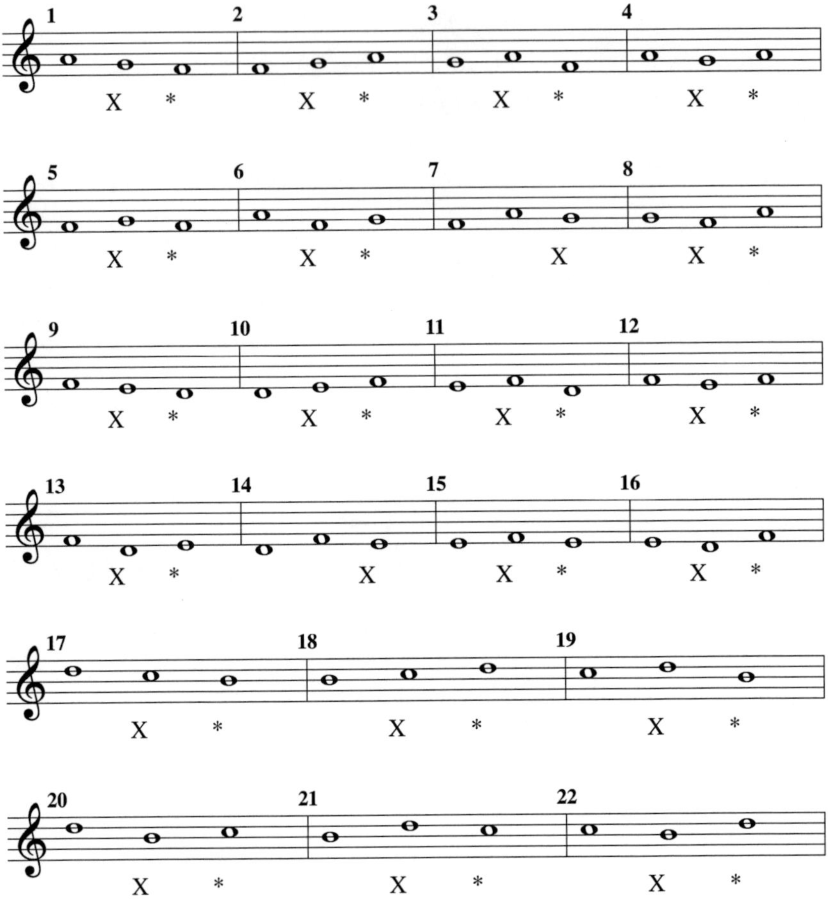

There are several factors over which we have no control: health, fatigue, mood, weather—temperature and humidity, and room acoustics; however, we do have control over a) posture (immediate); b) choral acoustical environment that aids in accurate hearing in rehearsals include multiple variations in seating positions (choral horseshoe design recommended, an arm-length between each singer; singers seated in mixed positions.)

Each rehearsal offers an opportunity to develop good ear/voice coordination, vowel uniformity, and continuous re-listening to overtones. Learn to hear especially low major 3rds.

COMPOSITIONAL STRUCTURE THAT AFFECTS INTONATION

Harmony

Dissonance, chromaticism, and key change directly impact singers' abilities to acquire accurate pitch consistently.

Melody

Attaining accurate pitch in singing whole-step/half-step scales ascending and descending must be a priority. Ascending scale intervals accumulate flat pitch because they are not quite wide enough. Descending scales consistently cause flat pitch because they are sung "under" the pitch.

Another source of acquiring flat pitch relates to singing descending major and minor thirds inaccurately. This relates to a combination of singing these intervals, over time slightly wide and also with inaccurate ear/voice coordination when landing on the descending note. Wide melodic leaps of 4ths, 5ths, 6ths, and 7ths, ascending and descending, especially create poor ear/voice coordination.

Rhythm

Slow (long) notes and fast (short) notes create flat pitch. Pitch sags when sustaining a long note. Fast notes prevent accurate ear/voice coordination.

Texture

There are numerous choral compositions in which individual vocal parts occur in a range or tessitura that may cause fatigue or inaccurate voice/ear coordination; sustained over time these melodic textures invite flat pitch. Changes in textures also create poor intonation: from clear/open textures to thick/closed textures, and with sudden shifts from high to low textures.

Expressive Components

Abrupt changes in dynamics or sustained crescendos and diminuendos cause poor ear/voice legato. Composers' markings of articulations, especially staccato and marcato create poor ear/voice coordination, especially in the context of leaping to a note. Singing legato over time sometimes creates vocal fatigue. Tempo changes: ritards seem similar to drooping pitch; accelerandos, depending upon speed, create the inability to sing pitches accurately.

REHEARSAL SUGGESTIONS THAT AID IN ESTABLISHING GOOD INTONATION

1. Sit in mixed positions: STAB; BATS; sit in a horseshoe C position, creating an *acoustical cup*. Mixed positions develop singer's independence, ears, and musicianship.
2. Place singers at one arm's-length apart, barely touching the shoulder of the next singer.
3. Rehearse in rooms with high ceilings, allowing for optimal clarity.
4. Match all vowels in vertical sonorities.
5. Insist on long-line, energy-filled, supported singing with upright posture.
6. Wean the chorus from the piano as early as possible.
7. Because singers learn "associated pitch problems" when sight-reading, pay attention throughout the learning stage to the accuracy of ear/voice coordination. Once the notes are well learned over time, change the key up or down a half step to alleviate many of the associated pitch problems acquired

during the note learning stage. A new key automatically requires vocal cord adjustments. Pitch automatically improves.

8. After notes are learned, avoid the keys of:

    F–sing on E or F♯ instead

    C–sing on B or C♯ instead

    B♭–sing on A or B instead

    E♭–sing on D or E instead

9. For best intonation sing in the keys of: F♯, E, C♯, or A; singing in the keys of G, D, or A♭ occasionally can cause faulty pitch.

10. Be consistently aware of mixed functions. Diminuendo or ritardando may cause flatting. Crescendo or accelerando may result in sharping. These habits are hard to break.

11. Long held notes tend to flat. Sing long held notes while slowly sharping slightly to maintain a true pitch center.

TIMBRE, SONORITY, VOWELS

DEFINITION AND OVERVIEW

No element in choral music has greater impact on timbre than text. The sound-continuum of shifting colors produced by the passing mosaics of sustained vowel sounds and vocal timbres significantly contribute to the beauty of the choral sound. To achieve a beautiful unified sound vocal timbres of each section must be unified with matched vowels. Matching vowels means to match the color sonority of each section to attain timbres of one color. When the timbre of each section is unified, pitch improves and the beauty of the vocal sound is enhanced.

Principles for Acquiring Matched Vowels

1. Listen for textual duets and trios on the same vowels. Clarify them with parallel phrasing and articulation and unified vowels.
2. At principal cadences, when each part all sing the same vowel, the pitch is unified. If all parts except one sing the same vowel, modify the vowel to help unify the sonority.
3. Vowels
   - In extreme ranges, modify vowels.
   - In homophonic textures match pure vowels
   - Identify diphthongs or other vowel combinations
4. Mark consonants to be voiced, unvoiced, heard, and silent. Remember voiced consonants (*m n v ng rr)* take more time.

Intensity and the Relationship to Structural and Expressive Components

Definition and Overview

Intensity relates to volume, focus of vocal tone, and color, and functions as an expressive element in music that coincides with dynamics, articulation, phrasing, rubato, and linear direction. Use of intensity can also clarify balance. Balance plays an extremely important role in projecting musical structure.

Expressive Components

Dynamics illuminate passing musical gestures, highlight expressive nuances, and to a greater degree than any other expressive agent, are a powerful force in emphasizing structure and balance.

Articulation enhances structural clarity and serves an expressive function as well. Through articulation words gain clarity. Consonants are projected, and strong-weak syllables are clarified. Sometimes the meaning of a word (as opposed to the syllabic accent) is felt more powerfully by emphasizing each syllable equally, an effect that draws the listener into experiencing the emotional quality of the word.

Phrasing sets into relief specific segments of a musical line often with articulation. In brief segments or note-groups, phrasing heightens expression; in long segments, phrasing enhances continuity and direction.

Rubato is produced through fluctuations in tempo. While duration is the primary means through which it is realized, shifts in intensity normally accompany rubato. Cadential structures are heightened when rubato momentarily draws the music behind the pulse, and dramatic gestures are energized as rubato temporarily pushes the music beyond the pulse. Ritards and accelerandos respectively achieve similar effects through changes of pulse. Passing events are often heightened by rubato, especially in the context of illuminating the musical line and harmonic color.[50]

Linear direction. Many styles of music gain expression by emphasizing musical line. Intensity of direction serves long line with dynamics and rubato. Subtle dynamics, articulation, and rubato can also highlight shorter lines.

When expressive functions are unified with intensity, they add to an arsenal of communicative tools that heighten, illuminate, and clarify musical meaning. Of the four elements of music, intensity most directly affects the expressive components of music making.

---

50 Throughout the history of choral music, *rubato* has been a consistent and natural source for expression, ranging in various degrees from Gregorian chant through twenty-first century choral music. A slowing or speeding up in ninth century chant is found in polyphony of the Renaissance to multi-types of *rubato* that occurred in works of the seventeenth and eighteenth centuries; by the nineteenth century new styles of *rubato* had evolved. See Richard Hudson's *Stolen Time: The History of Tempo Rubato*, Oxford University Press, 1994, reprinted 2004.

Dynamics

Clarifying Structure, Improving Balance, Enhancing Expression

While studying the score, marking the score, and preparing the ear for rehearsal, look for structural duets—vocal parts that go together. Realize if they are to balance, dynamic changes will be required. Differentiate each melodic component dynamically. Highlight melodies that contain the most important structural values. Notes that serve purely a filler or pedal function are less important; allow them to recede into the background.

Dynamics and Melody

Music making takes place *between* notes; this is where expressive elements occur. Realize that dynamics amplify musical nuance, even subtly, but always with some effect.

Challenge editors' marks. Make decisions through score study and historical practices.

In determining balance, make a distinction between melodies that carry the lead when harmonized vertically and those that are inherently equal, as in contrapuntal textures. Add dynamics (louder or softer) to create better vocal balance in homophonic textures.

In polyphonic and contrapuntal passages, distinguish primary melodies (head motifs, subjects, countersubjects) from filler notes (long notes or cadences that overlap a phrase). Assign filler notes softer dynamics to make clear more important vocal lines. Allow decay if not structurally important.

Dynamics and Harmony

Harmonic progressions, strong-weak, weak-strong; strong-stronger, weak-weaker, invite associative responses and dynamic change.[51]

The interaction of harmonic, melodic, and rhythmic motion produces "pivots of energy." The pivot is literally the point at which there is a "release" of energy; for example, at a V–I authentic cadence, add a *crescendo* and *diminuendo*. Plagal cadences (IV–I) typically require a *diminuendo*. These dynamics highlight the quality of the intended energy.

Music takes place in time. Releasing energy occurs after a build-up of the motion of energy; conversely, energy ebbs from a release. In this way, the dynamic motion of *arsis,* accompanies the arrival to *thesis,* the release of tension.

Dynamics are especially made clear through the expressive use of rubato.

Dynamics and Balance

Shifts in balance occur when textures change. For example, a momentary triad may result in a four-part texture when one part is doubled at the unison by another. Often these changes occur because of rules of voice leading and do not reflect the composer's intention to make one part louder than another. Be aware of this tendency. To attain an appropriate balance in this context, sing doubled unisons softer, especially if doubled unisons are held.

Balance consideration involves detailed score preparation for rehearsals:

1. Circle balance problems made evident by the range and tessitura of individual parts.

---

51 See Chapter 15 on the Expressive Power of Intervals

2. Circle crossed parts.

3. Study the importance of a note's function (is it a filler, a pedal, or an important part of the compositional fabric?). Mark dynamics to balance parts.

4. Build a hierarchy of dynamics around notes or phrases based upon their structural importance.

5. Low textures are harder to hear and clarify; high textures are fatiguing to sing. Circle exceptionally low or high passages; use dynamic modifications to clarify textures.

6. When textures change from horizontal to vertical, open to close, high to low, number of parts, unison doublings, range and tessitura, balance problems occur. Rebalance parts in texture changes.

7. When all elements of a composition are heard appropriately and clearly in balance, the composer's musical conception and the compositional structure are clarified.

Dynamics and Duration

Assign gradations of dynamics to phrases that are marked by the composer with the traditional signs of crescendo and diminuendo.

Mark long lines that ascend to "destination points" incrementally: *mp, mp+, mf, mf+, f.* Link these incremental dynamic changes to ensemble pulse.

Longer notes decay through entropy (loss of energy). Depending on the tempo and the length of a held note, mark dynamics above sustained notes to remind the singer to maintain vocal energy, counteracting the natural tendency to run out of breath. Entropy often produces flatting.

GENERAL COMMENTS

Seek primary sources or collected works editions to verify the original dynamics. Choose the most authoritative practical edition. Challenge the editor's dynamics, be sure they make sense.

Reevaluate the composer's dynamics:

1. Evaluate the choir's vocal make-up; determine if their collective vocal potential can realize the composer's dynamic intentions. If necessary, adjust the dynamics accordingly.
2. Evaluate the acoustics of the performance hall. Adjust dynamics accordingly.
3. Study the musical gesture first, and validate or change the composer's (or publisher's) markings.
4. Honor the composer's dynamics by understanding the reason behind them.

OBSERVED CHORAL TENDENCIES: SOPRANOS SHARP, ALTOS ARE SOFT, TENORS FLAT, BASSES ARE LATE

Sopranos sing in high ranges often through their vocal break. Especially with youthful or inexperienced voices, they tend to push, and sharp. Be aware of this tendency especially when sopranos sing from G to high G. The E natural frequently sharps.

Altos are hard to hear because their part is comparatively low. They are overbalanced by sopranos, high or overlapping parts of tenors, and strong basses in high ranges. Sacred music of the Renaissance, Baroque, and Classic eras were often sung by men or boys. Male voices sang alto parts either in falsetto or chest voice, depending on the range. Most likely they maintained the composer's intended balance.

Depending upon the balance, baritones can sing the alto part from low F to D. If the alto requires a higher range, tenors can reinforce from low G to high F. Some baritones and tenors also possess good falsettos that can offer well-blended strength for altos.

Tenors. A high-voice tenor is a rare treat. The vocal range and general tessitura of tenor parts (D to high A) are quite high for many tenors, especially over the vocal break F/F♯/G. Singing in that range becomes quite tiring. Fatigue invites flat pitch. Altos with strong low voices can greatly strengthen the tenor part in these ranges.

Basses sing low notes. Low notes vibrate slowly at low frequencies; they can be hard to hear and difficult to move quickly, thus basses often sing behind the beat. To aid the basses in keeping tempo, have them sing low notes separated with a semi-staccato approach. This technique reinforces quick ear/voice coordination and assists basses in singing low pitches in time with the whole ensemble.

SUMMARY

Marking the score imprints the mind and prepares the ear; in this way the musical materials are brought into consciousness in the conductor's mind's ear and serve as a foundation for listening in rehearsals. This process rivets the conductor's attention to the four elements of music—duration, pitch, timbre, and intensity—and sets an aural foundation for the rehearsal.

Preparing to listen for these elements is key to the conductor's success in implementing change. The score and the ear become one. In rehearsal, teach singers to understand the process they are using and how they serve the music. By making conscious the process choral singers use to acquire the conductor's mental-aural image, singers empower themselves develop pride in their abilities to master these skills. The pride they feel elicits cohesive and positive energy. Realizing the goal of inspired singing is the result of mastering these skills.

CHAPTER 10
THE EAR AND HOW TO LISTEN[52] ∿

Communicating mental-aural images to singers requires time, patience, discipline, and experience. The process is circular. The conductor measures the sound produced by the choir against her mental-aural image and feeds information back to the choir. The choir then reshapes the sound. As this process continues the choir's sound begins to match the conductor's mental-aural image. The ear is the channel through which sound information is transferred. The ear is the yardstick, the truth teller. The ear makes possible the conductor's ability to realize her conception.

The better the conductor's ear, the more effective it will be in attaining the conductor's mental-aural image. All information is gathered by the ear. The information received can be categorized by four musical elements: duration, pitch, timbre, and intensity. Each element contributes to the picture of the whole. The ear has the capacity to hear all four elements at the same time. The mind focuses selectively on one element at a time, but also has the capacity to focus on all informational levels simultaneously.

---

52   Ibid, chapter 16

Learning to hear on four levels requires natural aptitude, training, and experience. Each rehearsal presents a fresh opportunity to expand the ear's capacity. Concentration is the key. Conductors who concentrate reap the rewards of increased auditory perception to identify more quickly information related to duration, pitch, timbre, and intensity. As the ear improves, the conductor's ability to evaluate information improves, providing her with the necessary knowledge to implement change.

How to Listen[53]

Picture a dial. While the choir is singing, slowly turn the dial and focus your concentration on one element of music at a time. Spend considerable time listening to one element—*pitch,* for example. Quality, amplitude, accuracy, intonation, balance, dynamics, articulation, phrasing—all these characteristics may enter into your assessment of the choir's pitch.

Next, picture the dial and turn it to *timbre,* or a combination of both *pitch* and *timbre,* since these two elements can be closely related in function. Vowels, color, sonority, and texture are all facets of timbre. Then, listen for *duration.* This is a complex activity, because *duration* overlaps with *pitch, timbre,* and *intensity.* Specific aspects of listening to *duration* are linked inevitably to rhythmic accuracy, ensemble rhythm, tempo, metric structure, and to speed of harmonic rhythm. The expressive elements—*dynamics, phrasing, articulation, rubato,* and *linear direction*—are served by *duration* as well as *intensity.*

Now, turn the dial to *intensity.* Dynamics and color plus balance leap to mind. Focus on each *expressive element* of music by using "the dial" and listening for articulation, phrasing, line or rubato.

---

53   "Mastery," pp. 113–115.

Turning the dial focuses the conductor's auditory concentration on one element at a time. The capacity to hear increases when the conductor's energy is focused with full concentration in this way. Through repeated rehearsals a conductor builds an acute degree of auditory perception, and learns to hear more than one level for longer periods of time.

Conductors cannot listen too long without forgetting what they have heard. Keep track of each element that needs fixing as you measure the choir's sound against your mental-aural image. To avoid breaking the singers' concentration, do not stop to correct until you hear at least three problems, or more if your auditory memory can store them up. By vocal part, measure number, and beat, in that order, describe what you want to hear (positive). Verbally compare what your heard with what you want to hear (positive). Over time, this approach will provide the choir with positive incentives for *change*. If the "why" of "what you want" is clearly explained, you will provide the choir with invaluable positive imaging to accomplish your goals.

In summary, the conductor motivates the choir to give meaningful aural life to the written notation which represents the composer's conceptualization—her sound image.

While correcting specific aspects of a choir's singing, it is important to also confirm aspects you like! For example, "I like the way you shape the phrase in bars x-y-z, however, in the tenor part at bar x on beat 2, the G natural should be sung higher; mark it with an 'up' arrow. Basses, in bar y, beat 3, sing the eighth note quicker; it is late following the dotted quarter. Mark it with an arrow moving towards the next note. Altos, in bar z beat 4, sing more strongly. You are overbalanced in this texture. Mark the notes *mf* with a stress on each to give more presence. Sopranos in bar y, modify the 'ee' vowel, it is too bright in the high vocal range. Modify the vowel to 'ih' to give the sound more space. Choir, bars x–y–z continue to have an excellent line; make these individual modifications, and continue to sing with energy and purpose, and give dynamic shape to your individual parts."

Conductors can listen horizontally or vertically. *Both* types of listening open a conductor's ear to duration, pitch, timbre, and intensity. By thoroughly preparing the score, the ear, serves as a memory bell in rehearsal, and more importantly, the foundation upon which to organize the way we hear. Over time, by listening, measuring the choir's sound against the mental-aural image, and reshaping the sound, the choir's image of the music grows closer to the conductor's. When the profound experience of "matching conceptualization" occurs, *ensemble mastery* will result.

CHAPTER 11
REHEARSING[54] ⮞

INTRODUCTION

Rehearsing at the highest level of the choral art is a vastly complex yet very rewarding process. There is something uncanny about the rehearsal process—the ability to develop in choral singers a technical and musical concept of the score that matches that of the conductor's mental-aural image (the mind's ear). Developing matching conceptualizations is inspiring, often felt as spiritual. How does the conductor achieve this? By creating a *unanimous vision:* a *unity of ensemble.*

Rehearsals are the forum in which conductor and choir come together to engage in a creative process that is normally motivated by a concrete goal: performance. The quality of rehearsing is inevitably measured by the quality of performance. While disagreements concerning details of interpretation are as common as conductors are different, few listeners will fail to recognize an outstanding performance.

---

54 Concepts from "Mastery of Choral Ensemble," pp. 113–115.

Outstanding performances communicate. They allow listeners and participants to transcend their common daily experience. Outstanding performances enrich lives and rejuvenate spirits. Good rehearsals do the same thing. How can rehearsals best serve music's ultimate enriching and rejuvenating goal? By focusing the energy of singers on unifying the four elements of music. When the meaning of a composer's composition is revealed, *communication* occurs.

In the process of unifying the elements of music, the choir absorbs and assimilates a unanimous vision. This vision projected by the choir through ensemble unity clarifies the form, the function, and the design revealing the music's structure, reinforcing meaning and enhancing communication. It is through meaningful communication that music realizes its profound capacity to inspire. The results: *mastery of choral ensemble.*

It is important to point out that all of the principles upon which effective rehearsals are based require two essential ingredients: energy and desire. The energy the conductor gives is the primary motivator that stimulates singers to achieve the conductor's ideas. Singers must be motivated to accomplish the conductor's goals. The conductor, motivated by the quality of the music, the conceptual vision, and the joy received in realizing the conception, cannot help but project positive energy. Enthusiasm, encouragement, patience, humor, and positive reinforcement will serve the conductor well when singers are engaged in the rehearsal process.

REHEARSAL PREPARATION

In rehearsal, each element of the conductor's preparation is drawn together. The conductor begins his preparation by studying the score. Score study and stylistic insight stimulate a mental-aural image. The rehearsal provides the context in which the mental-aural image is realized. Through the ear, the conductor measures the choral sound against his mental-aural image and implements *change*. How does the conductor draw choral singers toward the compelling image he possesses? How does he create a *unanimous* vision, a *unity of ensemble*? The answer is by rehearsing (re-hear-sing).

No aspect of the conductor's process directly affects the performance more than the conductor's ability to rehearse. Without effective rehearsing, insights into the score will not be realized. No matter how well the conductor is able to hear, no matter how visionary his interpretation, no matter how highly communicative his conducting technique is, the principal foundation upon which the actualization of the score rests is *rehearsing*.

Chapter 9, "Preparing the Ear for Listening and the Score for Rehearsing," provides analytical information concerning the principal elements of music: duration, pitch, timbre, and intensity. Rehearsals provide the opportunity to unify these four elements. In this process of unifying, the choir absorbs and assimilates a unanimous vision—a unity of ensemble.

The interaction of the four elements of music and the expressive components (explicit and implicit in notational symbols)—dynamics, phrasing, articulation, linear direction and rubato— creates the conductor's mental-aural image. This breadth of preparation and insight arms the *ear* of the conductor. He is now ready to rehearse – *re-hear* by *listening,* carefully measuring his mind's ear against the choir's sound. Each time, rehearsals offer the synthesis of the mental-aural image, the ear, and rehearsing: the core of the conductor's process. Based upon these principles above are the following practical suggestions to be considered during the rehearsal process.[55]

---

55   *Mastery of Choral Ensemble*, 95.

STAGES OF LEARNING

There are many stages of learning. If each piece or movement of a large work is at a different stage of development, singers' energies can be rejuvenated by contrasting the varied musical demands. To organize these stages group compositions into two categories: musical and technical, and three stages: preliminary, technical, and final.

In the *preliminary stage*, singers get to know a composition. This first stage opens a window into why the composer set the text in a particular way, which provides a meaningful context for teaching the notes, the rhythms, and the text.

The *technical stage* teaches the choir to sing the notes in tune with matched vowels, in balance, and rhythmically aligned, developing choral ensemble. This technical stage of ensemble development represents seventy-five percent of the work.[56] In the technical stage, separate words from music. Do this early in the rehearsal process because text impinges upon pitch, duration, timbre, and intensity.

The *final stage* overlays expressive qualities introduced in the preliminary stages with the ensemble development achieved in the technical stage. The inherent expressive qualities (the *affetti)* can now be fully developed, integrating them with the foundation of ensemble pitch, rhythm, and balance.

Make clear singers are expected to mark their parts during these musical stages. They soon realize that being a part of an ensemble is a privilege that requires responsibilities. When singers feel responsible for marking their individual part, they are empowered with the ability and knowledge to effectively improve and maintain *change,* the core of the rehearsal process.

---

56   See chapters 8–11 for rehearsal techniques on intonation, vowels, balance, and ensemble rhythm.

So that singers do not learn faulty intonation and imprecise rhythmic habits during the initial sight-reading note-learning stage, correct the pitch and rhythmic alignment throughout this early stage. Pitch problems arise from the subtle ear/voice coordination required in finding the right note. After learning the right notes, singers frequently fail to maintain proper pitch. When poor associative pitch habits continue, singers invariably and unconsciously perpetuate these habits long after the notes are learned. During the initial stage, constantly correct the notes, intonation, rhythms, and the alignment of rhythms.

INTONATION

To develop ensemble intonation employ the following tactics. After notes are secure, sing them on a brief staccato "doo." Do not allow "doo" with accents.[57] Insist on a pure "oo" vowel, not the diphthong in words like "you" or "due." Once choral singers can sing semi-staccato "doo" in tune together, and in balance, and can then sing legato "doo" by connecting the notes;[58] add text.

RHYTHM

Ensemble rhythm is the foundation of duration, pitch, balance, timbre, intensity, and the expressive elements. There are a number of techniques that can help sensitize singers to ensemble rhythm. In my experience, a unanimous group pulse is best achieved by feeling group pulse silently. Energy harnessed together in silence produces

---

57 The "doo" sung as staccato must be voiced long enough to allow accurate pitch by maintaining good ear/voice coordination. I often refer to this as "legato doo with space/silence between notes."

58 "Oo" used for too long a period of time can produce vocal fatigue. Change to "nah" in legato contexts, and/or move on to another piece that is at different rehearsal stage.

unanimous group pulse. Ask singers to count the basic pulse silently. Each singer then feels the pulse individually. At a pre-designated point, ask singers to clap at their point of arrival. It is surprising how each singer measures time. Try this technique several times so singers learn to concentrate on pulse during silence. When unanimous ensemble pulse occurs, singers exalt in their measured unison clap.

To achieve clarity of ensemble rhythm, consider the following. Have the choir sing "staccato doo" or "pum" (sustaining the "m"). Inaccuracies are clearly shown when "doo" or "pum" occur at the wrong time. Count-singing by subdividing the beat, is a technique that highlights phrasing and builds unanimous group pulse.

These techniques help sensitize singers to ensemble pulse, however, when text is added, group pulse is affected. Consonants take time. They affect vertical and horizontal alignment. Be alert that ensemble rhythm may slow down. To combat slowing, sing correct rhythms, vowels, and consonants on a pitch a 4th (F, B♭, E♭, A♭) or 5th apart. This procedure aids ensemble rhythm by focusing the singers' attention on the alignment of rhythm and text, taking away temporarily their own melodic line, only the rhythms.

ENSEMBLE TENDENCIES AND SUGGESTIONS

Do not allow singers to mix functions. For example, slowing down on a diminuendo contains an associative tendency of flatting. Counteract these tendencies by separating functions. Sing a diminuendo while sharping the pitch, or speed up the tempo during a diminuendo. Remind singers of associative tendencies in rehearsal.

Avoid singing in extreme dynamic ranges until notes and rhythms are secure. Soft dynamics require focused breath control and invite flat pitch. Loud dynamics sung for considerable time invite vocal forcing and fatigue. Rehearse at a comfortable level, *mp–mf*. Later, incorporate proper dynamics.

After the notes and expressive gestures are learned, transpose the key a half step up or down. This modifies the physiological association of how the notes feel in the voice when sung in the original key. This technique counteracts many of the associative pitch problems that have accrued over time.

Practical Hints: The key of F major frequently goes flat when continuously used. After the fundamental stages of learning are complete in *a cappella* compositions, change the key to F♯ or E depending upon vocal balance and color considerations. The key of C often flats; change to C♯ or B. Compositions in B♭ can flat; change the key to B or A. Minor keys of d, a, and g often flat. Change to the minor keys of c♯, a♯, or f♯.

If singers tire or lose concentration in rehearsal, energy is the key. Stand up, move, exercise, be humorous, offer positive support and enthusiasm. Take a break! Rehearse in rooms that have clear non-reverberant acoustics yet with reasonable room ambience. Avoid rooms with low ceilings, acoustic tile, rugs, curtains, and acoustical shells with low panels.

Sit and stand in positions that allow singers to take responsibility for their own pitch, rhythm, and balance without interference from other singers on the same part. In rehearsals and concerts sing in mixed quartets, for example STAB or BATS. These positions help singers acquire good individual intonation and independent rhythmic security. Singing in mixed parts, especially in polyphonic textures, develops independence and musicianship.

Singers often hear best when facing each other. They especially hear well in a C-shaped horseshoe position that creates an acoustical cup. Even outdoors, singing in a horseshoe position allows singers to hear better. To attain a high degree of clarity when standing or sitting in a C-shaped position, create space of about one arm's length between singers. This position also applies when an acoustic shell is used.

At the initial rehearsal stage the piano may be used to facilitate note learning; however, as soon as possible wean singers from dependence on the piano. The sound of the piano[59] greatly affects the ability of singers and conductors to accurately hear correct intonation, rhythm, balance, and diction. When the piano doubles all parts, singers tend not to listen to other parts.

Summary

The joy singers experience in singing with an inspired conductor is transformed into a collective energy that replenishes and inspires both conductor and singer. This mutual rehearsal experience is one of the highest rewards of the Conductor's Process.

A common thread of energy runs through each component of the Conductor's Process, especially in the remarkable interrelationship of the core elements: the mental-aural image, the ear, and the rehearsal. Discovering the richness and depth of a profoundly crafted masterpiece is an extremely exhilarating experience. This compelling process inspires the conductor to imagine the music in performance. Through analyzing the structure and style of the work, a powerful image of the score emerges, igniting a sound-vision that energizes the

---

59   The piano is tuned to equal temperament to accommodate the Pythagorean flaw. The Pythagorean flaw is a term this author uses for a natural acoustical phenomenon. It is measured by the audible pitch difference between the "E" overtone produced by the fundamental pitch "C" at the frequency ratio of 5:4, and the "E" produced by tuning a series of perfect 5ths (C–G–D–A–E) at the frequency ratio of 3:2. The comparative pitch difference between the two E's is easily heard; one only need to tune two ranks of an organ or harpsichord to these temperaments to hear the flaw. It is not subtle.

conductor and motivates the choir. The choir in turn is inspired by the informed impassioned energy emanating from the conductor.

In rehearsal, as the conductor and choir build an ensemble that projects a unity of conception through a unity of presentation, spirits soar as they work together to perfect the process of the multifaceted art of recreating music. Mastery results. The beauty of the music inspires, rejuvenates, and enriches the lives of the participants in performance by projecting collective vision. The choir realizes the conductor's vision, and together they are rejuvenated in a cycle of energy that emanates from the process itself. Thus, energy is the catalyst for making music transcendent, and for breathing spirituality into the interaction of humanity and music.

PART III:
SPECIAL TOPICS

CHAPTER 12

PAINTING WITH WORDS: VERBS AND OTHER PARTS OF SPEACH ⮴

Catalysts for Emotional Expression

Choral directors use two words to describe the relationship of visual and aural art that relates to how a composer sets text: *word painting*. To represent sound images, composers employ these elements of music: harmony (consonance, dissonance), melody (shape, direction), rhythm (fast, slow), and texture (polyphonic, homophonic). While a composer's conceptions transmit the aural representation of his ideas, it seems odd that "painting" is used to describe these aural events.

Throughout my many years of studying scores and preparing rehearsals, it occurred to me that there were a number of common predispositions that drew composers towards word painting. Highlighting words with expressive musical vocabularies were the result of their desire to aurally represent parts of speech. Verbs seem especially enticing, for they express both motion and emotion, qualities abundant in sacred and secular texts.

Notational portrayal of feelings and moods appeared in the sixteenth century sparked first in Josquin des Prez's motets. By the middle of the sixteenth century, word painting in the madrigal became the catalyst for the *seconda pratica,* especially in the hands of Cipriano de Rore and Giaches de Wert, and confirmed in the madrigals of their brilliant student Claudio Monteverdi. Concurrent with the development of the madrigal, "eventually performers applied expressive elements not included in the notation, such as dynamics and tempos. In response to the emotion of the text, mid-sixteenth-century performers are described as singing fast, slow, soft, and loud."[60] While very few expression marks were written by composers during the seventeenth century, [61] the emotional quality of verbs, nouns, adjectives, even personal pronouns and conjunctions became subject to amplification by the composer from the seventeenth century to today.

Increasingly, throughout the eighteenth century, composers used Italian words primarily to describe changes in tempo and dynamics. Composers added markings when they were no longer the only one who performed their works. Expressive marks in increasing detail flourished throughout the nineteenth century to today. In sum, from 1350 to 1700 there was no need for composers to write expression marks into choral scores because contemporaries understood how the notation reflected the intended inherent expression. Over the last 300 years, it is clear composers became increasingly adamant about telling us "how it goes," represented by written instructions they surmise will guide us to the correct interpretation.

---

60 Hudson, *Stolen Time,* 6

61 In the 1648 publication of Heinrich Schütz's *Geistliche Chor-Music,* of the 29 motets, there appears in *Ich Weiss, das mein Erlöser lebt,* the word *Tarde,* written by Schütz as an indication to "slow down" at the end of this composition.

In this context, an important question to ask is, "what *part of speech* is the composer emphasizing; what emotion is he trying to highlight and by what element of music, harmony, melody, rhythm, texture or a combination?" The notation may not offer detailed meaning; it may simply convey a general mood or the emotional meaning behind the notational symbols.

In writing this book, I have explored many interrelated subjects that relate to emotion, those made explicit by the notation or by expressive marks, and those implied by the contextual congruence of the elements of music: harmony, melody, rhythm, and texture. Because choral compositions *reflect* to some degree or another word-music relationships, it is important to consider the word "reflect." In that context, two questions arise: "how does the composer *reflect* the text?" and *"why* did he make those specific choices?" "Why" and "how" directly reflect a composer's prioritization of what *feelings* drew him to a specific word or a phrase.

Connecting a composer's *reflections* to a specific part of speech is key. Verbs, for example, signal *motion* and *emotion*. Composers highlight verbs of *motion* primarily with movement: fast notes, direction of notes, tempo changes. They occur especially in polyphonic or fugal textures. Composers highlight verbs of *emotion* with harmony: fear, sadness, disappointment, loss, and anxiety with dissonance, chromaticism, minor chords, cross-relations, close textures, and unresolved progressions; happiness, joy, exuberance, love, freedom, and contentment with major keys, major chords, modal progressions, harmonic motion, open textures, and high or clear textures.

A composer's expressive vocabulary (explicit and implicit) piques my interest and always causes me to ask, "what nuances can my choir apply to clarify the composer's thinking?" The vocabulary of emotional expression, word painting by parts of speech, is made relevant only when choirs can meaningfully project it aurally. In rehearsal, conductors teach singers how to project emotional expression by analyzing a composer's notation—the form, structure, harmony, melody, rhythm, and texture—that reveals the emotional connection to varied parts of speech.

The application of expressive nuances we choose requires thought and perspective: "what *is* the composer trying to say?" A composer's vocabulary of feelings is also intertwined with the expressive power of intervals.[62] Intervals, both vertical and horizontal, convey moods, interact with parts of speech, and enhance emotional flavors. In the words of a most interesting book by Don Campbell, "Pure basic emotions. . . are most potent in the composer's hands, engendering music which we often consider most moving and beautiful."[63]

In considering the many stimuli that trigger a composer's written vocabulary of expressive nuances, I offer interpretive ideas of two well-known works by the mid-sixteenth-century composer Giovanni Pierluigi da Palestrina, and the early seventeenth-century composer Heinrich Schütz.[64] Below is an analysis of Palestrina's motet "Sicut cervus desiderat" (Prima pars). The analysis of Palestrina's expressive gestures present patterns of insight that illuminate the composer's musical rhetoric. These "handles of expression" illustrate what expressive gestures can be applied to highlight the emotional meaning of a specific word or a phrase of text.

---

62   A thorough discussion of the expressive power of intervals occurs in the final chapter of the book.

63   Don Campbell, *Music: Physician for Times to Come*; p. 133

64   Schütz's *Selig sind die Toten* is analyzed in the Appendix.

PALESTRINA: *SICUT CERVUS DESIDERAT*

Palestrina, *maestro di cappella* of the Cappella Giulia at St. Peter's Basilica from 1551–1554 and from 1571–1594, when he composed *Sicut cervus* for the Cappella Giulia. It was published in 1584. *Sicut cervus desiderat* requires attention to many expressive nuances to bring audible clarity to Palestrina's word painting: tempo, tuning, phrasing, articulation, dynamics, linear direction, rubato, and balance.

OVERVIEW

The text, based on Psalm 42:1, is divided into three overlapping sections: 1) *Sicut cervus desiderat ad fontes aquarum* (As the deer desires running waters, mm. 1–25); 2) *ita desiderat* (so longs (for), 24–44); and 3) *anima mea, ad te Deus* (my soul for you, God, 40–58). The central theme is the verb *desiderat* (longs for, desires). Although "desires" appears only twice in the Psalms, Palestrina amplifies the emotional meaning by repeating "desiderat" twenty-four times.

WORD-MUSIC RELATIONSHIPS RELATED TO STRUCTURE

The verb "desiderat" has three complementary meanings: to desire, to long for, to yearn. Palestrina makes clear this thematic message in mm. 1–25 with short rhythmic ascending notes that contrast with long flowing lines ("running waters"), melismatic motion for only the two words "ita desiderat" in mm. 23–44, and the object of *desire* "my soul, for you, God," mm. 40–58. "Anima mea," (my soul) the object of "desiderat," is set with a motif of five imitative descending notes, each enhanced with an appoggiatura—a *longing* gesture. The sopranos first sing the motive on the highest note of the motet. The three words "ad te, Deus" are extended with ornamental lines that highlight the noun "Deus."

Palestrina describes running water with continuous overlapping polyphonic lines, interrupted by two structural cadences (mm. 22 and 55) and two inconsequential passing cadences (mm. 13 and 17). The specific word "desiderat," set in quarter notes, dotted quarters, and eighth notes, gains increasing urgency. The subtle poignancy of Palestrina's conception for urgency is manifested by the fact there are no structural cadences in two-thirds of the motet (mm. 23–55), reinforcing Palestrina's conception "my soul urgently desires God." Passing dissonances (major 2nds or minor 7ths) are common. Palestrina paints nouns (water, deer, fountain) with major 7th dissonances, highlighted in my edition with vertical slanting lines. The dissonances appear at two phrygian cadences (mm. 10 and 37), reflecting emotions of pain and sadness related entirely to yearning.

Given these insights into Palestrina's score, how can we best make clear these inherent compositional gestures? The basic principles to best aurally amplify the expressive meaning of this motet are to balance contrapuntal lines and tune dissonance and principal cadences. The emotional meaning of parts of speech (nouns, verbs, and so on) can be created with dynamics, phrasing, articulation, linear direction, and rubato.

Dynamics

When performing *Sicut cervus,* dynamics can be employed on many levels.
1. In sections one and two to clarify long and short notes of the head-motifs and subsequent quick notes on "desiderat," add crescendos and diminuendos.

2. As each vocal part ascends (to allow listeners to perceive points of arrival) create a forward motion crescendo.

3. At the end of the first section, the bass entrance overlaps the structural cadence with the head motif, *ita desiderat* mm. 23–43. This twenty-bar section magnifies the word "desire" with ever-flowing, overlapping, quick polyphonic lines. By employing subtle dynamics with forward motion, there will be an increased feeling of urgency telegraphed by the continuous motion. Take care to balance quicker notes with longer cadential or "filler" notes by allowing long notes to recede into the background.

Palestrina signals each structural (and passing) cadence with suspensions—a structural announcement. To clarify the signal, balance the two-note suspensions. In the third section, *Anima mea,* Palestrina also consistently announces the head-motive with a suspension, enhancing the emotional quality of "my soul" (possessive adjective, noun), the object of "desiring." The suspensions feel "imploring." In this context, that emotion is best served by adding a brief crescendo with excellent tuning and balancing the two notes of the appoggiatura.

It is interesting to observe that the last third of the motet contains few eighth notes. This pattern seems to suggest a quality of contemplation ("my soul for thee, God"). A *poco* diminuendo can highlight this emotion. The final cadence occurs before the last four bars (a typical trait of many Palestrina's motets). The motet concludes with a deliberate feeling of winding down, enhanced by the final plagal cadence. It can be served appropriately by an expressive diminuendo.

PHRASING

In my edition (shown at the end of this chapter), micro phrase-groups are indicated with brackets placed above three-note groupings. The purpose of these marks is to visualize the melodic and rhythmic asymmetric grouping of each vocal line. Normal two-note groupings of motives relate to the natural half-note pulse signaled by the ¢ *alla breve* sign. The bracket, placed above three-note groupings reveal asymmetry and highlight the melodic-rhythmic nuances of each independent vocal part, a primary source of *expression* in singing Renaissance polyphony. To highlight asymmetric polyphonic phrase groups add a subtle rubato with dynamic fluctuations.[65]

MOTION AND RUBATO

As Don Campbell writes in *Music: Physician for Times to Come,* "Music moves. Not only emotionally, but bodily: music dances inwardly and incites to gesture, to dance, outwardly.

Song and gesture both contain movement generated by the musical thought and form . . . Even thinking music, without sound, involves the experience of movement in imagination . . . the movement of music thought is not mere movement: it is expressive movement."[66] Notation is a graph that visually indicates pitch and time.

When a choir sings motion occurs naturally; music-making and motion are thus allied. Shifts from two-note to three-note groupings commonly occur in polyphonic textures and in hemiolas and phrases that mirror the strong-weak syllabication of words. These shifts offer modest opportunities for illumination with rubato and dynamics, creating subtle expressivity.

---

65 0 See Chapter 14 on Renaissance Choral Performance that describes specific techniques for highlight triple and duple groupings.

66 Ibid, Campbell, 124

Quick-moving notes reflect verbs of motion, or emotion. Forward motion will aid in this emotional *affect*. As the phrase ends, relaxation will occur. Melodic lines that arrive at a momentary destination, as demonstrated in the opening motive, rise and fall according to the syllabic stress of the words: *Sicut* **cer**-*vus* de-*si*-*der*-*at ad* **fon**- *tes* a-**qua**-*rum*. Cadences indicate how the composer organizes the textual structure. Modest motion of tempo articulates the beginning or end of a musical structure. To highlight cadences add rubato to unwind the forward motion (mm. 22–23, 54–55), and especially at the final cadence. As Hudson says in *Stolen Time: The History of Tempo Rubato,* "ritarding at cadences seems to have been transmitted also to polyphonic music. Late in the sixteenth century the cadence could be emphasized . . . by extending the penultimate note or chord."[67]

Below is my edition of Palestrina's *Sicut cervus desiderat*. The original pitch was F; I transposed it up one whole tone to G[68]. The original note values are halved. Brackets above notes indicate three-note groupings in the context of duple meter. Cadences and dissonances are projected by vertical and slanted dotted lines.

---

67   Ibid, Campbell, 124

68   Most interestingly, the pitch of the organ of Cappella Giulia was a half-step low to A=440. The sound of Palestrina's *Sicut cervus* was therefore pitched on F#, a "key" that corresponds easily to falsetto or high tenor range as well as tenors, baritones, basses. The Harvard Glee Club performed *Sicut cervus* on F# many times and it created a beautiful and natural sound.

Sicut cervus desiderat
Prima pars

Giovanni Pierluigi da Palestrina
(c.1525-1594)

Edited for the Harvard-Radcliffe Collegium Musicum by Jameson Marvin

Psalm 42: verse 1 *As the hart desires springs of water, so longs my soul for thee, O God.*
(As the deer longs for running waters, so my soul longs for you, my God)

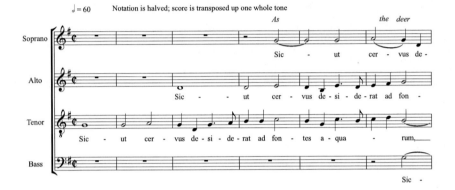

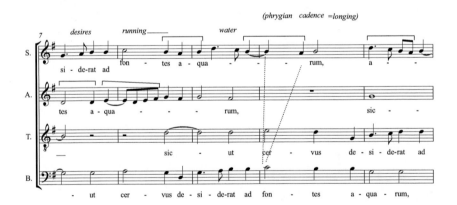

CHAPTER 13
PERFORMING RENAISSANCE
CHORAL MUSIC ∾

WHY PERFORM RENAISSANCE CHORAL MUSIC TODAY?

There can be little doubt about music's profound capacity to rejuvenate spirits. Moments of mourning and rejoicing have elicited group-song, connecting the collective cathartic spirits of participants. One of the enriching experiences of performing quality choral literature from the vast treasure-trove of the western choral tradition is that the cumulative experience provides insight into cultural and aesthetic values of past eras. Choral music of the Renaissance offers an enormous panoply of styles and genres of unsurpassed beauty, astonishing complexity, and expressive depth. Eternal truths are found in this music, truths that when revealed can provide solace, just as they did hundreds of years ago. Why does performing sacred Renaissance choral music offer a contemplative spirituality, an inspiring experience that enlightens and rejuvenates?

I believe the answer lies in the very elements of this music that engender a transcendent quality for which we yearn. This quality is inherent in the compositional process. The texture of Renaissance motets and masses is primarily polyphonic, each vocal line is independent. The linear contours of each part are characterized by subtle asymmetric and independent units of long and short notes, a style derived from the melismas of Gregorian chant. Singing vocal lines expressively requires thought and concentration. The subtle dynamic-rhythmic nuances of Gregorian-chant phrasing demand attention. Shaping independently moving melodic lines of four or more parts, while at the same time maintaining vertical alignment through attention to ensemble rhythm, is both demanding and deeply satisfying. Performing Renaissance music well challenges the intellect, demands good musicianship, and elicits strong emotional responses.

The most compelling aspect of Renaissance polyphony is the composite process engenders a feeling of timelessness, a profound sense of the eternal. Multiple levels of independent rhythmic activity, combined with the relatively slow-moving harmonic rhythm, and the influence of mode, create an ethereal, other-worldly spirituality, an almost dream-like *affect*. The primary modes (dorian D-d, phrygian E-e, lydian F-f, mixolydian G-g) exert a powerful influence on the listener. Each mode has a particular sound-color, evinces moods, and reflects special qualities. The *affect* (the sound color) of each mode evokes immediate feelings.

Composers sought to match the *affect* of the mode to the *affect* of the text. Masses and motets with serious texts are frequently set in the dorian mode. Laments, lamentations, requiems, and chansons on sad texts often are composed in the phrygian mode. Motets and madrigals with provocative or passionate texts may appear in the lydian mode. Works with more frivolous, lightweight texts are set in the mixolydian mode. The intrinsic power of the mood of each mode is extremely compelling, and human emotions are stirred subconsciously by that power. Mood and mode are related. The word "mood" comes from "mode."

Chord progressions, inherent in the intervallic relationships of each mode evoke an ethereal, timeless quality, a "neither here nor there" effect, an emotion many experience as euphoria. Timelessness is projected when one vocal line contains a *cantus firmus* in long notes—a common structural practice in Renaissance music. Harmonies move slowly, and the *cantus firmus* is heard in relief against the simultaneous, independently moving vocal parts. The composite polyphonic texture projects multiple levels of time, evoking an otherworldly quality. The sound continuum is compelling. Performers and listeners are drawn into contemplation, to a place of quietness, a place where souls are refreshed and spirits revived.

These values are eternal. In hearing music of eternal value we are inspired to keep alive the transcendent qualities that confirm our humanity. The eternal we experience in performing sacred Renaissance music lifts us above our daily concerns. We experience this gift in rehearsal, and performance, just as Renaissance citizens did hundreds of years ago.

RENAISSANCE THEORY AND THE PHILOSOPHICAL FOUNDATIONS OF *PERFECTION* AND *NATURALNESS*[69]

Note values were principally the longa, breve, semibreve (the modern whole-note), minim (half-note), semi-minim (quarter-note), fusa (eighth-note), and semi-fusa (sixteenth-note) in use by the mid- to

---

69   A particularly good source on Renaissance notational theory appears in Allan Atlas's *Renaissance Music: Music in Western Europe, 1400-1600.* Some of the information above is derived in part from this author's monograph entitled *Perfection and Naturalness, A Practical Guide to the Performance of Renaissance Choral Music,* published by Oxford University Press in 2001. This author has revised and corrected some of his previous concepts and they are spread throughout this chapter with verbiage rephrased to accommodate the chapter's formatting.

late-sixteenth century. There were no meter signatures; if numbers were used they represented proportional relationships rather than beats per bar. There were no barlines, no ties, and no beamed notes. Each part was read by itself, with no visual knowledge of what the other parts were doing. Singers read their parts by holding their part book or by reading from a large manuscript placed in front of the choir with each vocal part still separated from one another. Composers used primarily C clefs and F clefs, and text underlay was inconsistent especially in manuscripts.

Expressive communication in singing Renaissance music rests upon the philosophical foundations of *Perfection and Naturalness*. Medieval and Renaissance theorists ascribed degrees of perfection to specific intervals according to their mathematical proportions. The unison (acoustically a 1:1 proportion) was the most perfect – the symbol of the one God, from which all other intervals followed. The octave (2:1) was the next simplest, and therefore the next most perfect (closest to God) – equivalent to the Christian theological figures God the Father and God the Son. The fifth (3:2) introduced the number three, which complete the Christian symbolism by invoking the Holy Trinity for Father, Son, and Holy Spirit.

EXPRESSIVE STYLE IN RENAISSANCE CHORAL PERFORMANCE

THE PRIMARY FOUNDATION: TUNING, TEMPO, PHRASING, DYNAMICS

From the early generations represented by Dufay, Ockeghem, and Josquin, through the era of Palestrina, Lassus, and Byrd, to the remarkable transitional works of Monteverdi and Schütz, certain underlying values and assumptions constitute a common vocabulary of expression. These values hold the key to bringing alive choral music of the Renaissance today.

These are the concepts of *Perfection and Naturalness* that relate to expressive singing and directly affect four basic elements of musical performance: tuning, tempo, phrasing, and dynamics. These components inherently relate to the expressive power of intervals[70]. Intervals project sound *affects* (moods and emotions). When we reveal these inherent emotions, performance becomes *authentic*. We realize in sound the composer's concept, the mental-aural image represented by the symbolic notation on the page. Simply put, intervals create moods and emotional responses.

Below are suggestions and perspectives on choral performance practice and stylistic values of the Renaissance.

TUNING

Pitch, Modes, Hexachords, Tuning—Temperament and Intervals

Pitch was not standard and varied greatly for choirs according to organ tunings; transposition from written pitch was normal. Singers read their vocal lines using *hexachord solmization syllables: ut, re, mi, fa, sol, la*. There were three hexachords that overlapped these six-note scales: C and G, or C and F if there was a flat in the key signature. Key signatures contained no sharps and had at most two flats; one flat transposed the mode up a 4th. Composers wrote accidentals in vocal parts often to highlight text music relationships. Performers added accidentals guided by "singers' rules" related to solmization syllables. (For more details about this, see the section at the end of this chapter.) While no signs of expression appear in Renaissance music, composers were usually the *maestro di cappella* of their choir and likely led them toward their desired expression.

---

70   Read chapter 15.

The eight-note scales of the church modes were the precursors of the organization of pitches that we now call "keys." *Modes* are normally revealed by the melodic outline and range of the tenor part and the descending note to the *finalis* of the mode, at cadences. The primary modes are: *Dorian* (D–d) which contains the sadness of *d, e, f* (minor), and the joy of *g, a, b* (major); thus *Dorian* is a "mixed mode": it sounds rather serious, thoughtful. *Phrygian* (E–e) has a very distinct sound, created by the half-step descending from f to e that sounds sad, mournful, imploring. *Lydian* (F–f) is arresting; play F scales over and over without B♭. It feels entirely unresolved, a sense of other worldliness—exotic, filled with tension, even quasi-erotic. *Mixolydian* (G–g) is a much "happier" sounding mode often setting "fa-la-la" madrigals. (See the end of this chapter for more information.)

Tuning relates to the philosophies of *perfection* and *naturalness,* most specifically to the Renaissance concept of temperament derived from the discussion above on "perfect intervals." Learning to hear and to sing pure intervals—unison, octave, perfect 5th, and M 3rd—are the key ingredients for tuning choirs today. All intervals, horizontal and vertical, create moods, especially when sung in tune. Accidentals often create intonation problems—those written by the composer or sung by the singer in the application of *musica ficta,* "false music." Singers applied chromatic changes according to various rules derived from using hexachord solmization when reading.

The typical temperament is Mean Tone tuning based on the overtone series of pure unisons, octaves, 5ths, and Major 3rds.[71]

---

71   Early Renaissance theorists still considered pure intervals to be the unison, octave, and fifth (the finals of Medieval cadences), and "left out the third." As the compositional style of early Renaissance composers flourished, and polyphony became the norm, more major 3rds appeared in vertical chords [M 3rds are heard readily in the overtone series especially in reverberant cathedrals.] By the middle of the 15th century especially English composers began to favor including the M 3rd at final cadences.

From this point of view we come into contact with the concepts of *perfect* and *imperfect* intervals. *Perfect intervals* are unison, octave, 5th, 4th, major 3rd; *imperfect intervals* are minor 3rd, major 6th, major/minor 2nd and 7th; augmented 4th and diminished 5th.

PRACTICAL APPLICATIONS—TUNING

Transpose Renaissance works to fit your choir's makeup; this was a Renaissance practice!

Tune intervals to the overtone series with major 3rds (mean tone tuning) and perfect 5ths (Pythagorean tuning). Major 3rds are low in comparison to equal temperament; perfect 5ths are slightly high in comparison to equal temperament. Sing *ascending* half and whole-steps *wide*; sing *descending* half and whole-steps *narrow*. By doing so, we borrow from the intervals of both Pythagorean and Mean Tone tuning systems.

MUSICA FICTA, CADENCES, AND HEXACHORDS

Musica vera ("true music") represents the notes and accidentals the composer wrote. *Musica ficta* ("false music") was created by a performer who sang an unwritten sharp or a flat to create a cadence, and is used today by editors to create cadences.

Imperfect major 6ths and minor 3rds in the score create cadences by resolving to perfect 8ves or unisons. We hear the "imperfection" by experiencing major 6ths and minor 3rds as intervals of tension— they "require" resolution. Cadences by composers or editors clarify the structure. Editors create cadences using *musica ficta* to widen a minor 6th to a major 6th (which resolves to an octave) or by narrowing a major 3rd to a minor 3rd (which resolves to a unison).

Other reasons for the employment of *musica ficta* by performers or by editors relate to avoiding tritones (*"diabolus in musica"*), harmonic or especially melodic, or when a harmonic tritone is doubled. (More details are given at the end of the chapter.)

TACTUS, PULSE, TEMPO, NOTATION, PROPORTIONS, GENRE AND STYLE EVOLUTION

Rhythmic notation in the fifteenth and sixteenth centuries, called mensural notation, was similarly based upon concepts of perfection and naturalness. In mensural notation, the number three—exemplified in Christian theology by the Holy Trinity—was depicted by the circle, universally understood as to represent the concept of oneness and completeness. The complete down-and-up motion of the choirmaster's arm indicated the actual speed of the *tactus*.[72] Renaissance theorists related the speed of the musical pulse, or *tactus,* to the most natural human pulse—"the heartbeat of a quietly breathing man," according to Franchino Gafori's *Practice Musicae* (Milan, 1496). The speed of the tactus was related to the breve (whole note). Most modern editions halve the notation; in halving the notation, the tempo relates to the half note.

Typical pulse is about 60 MM (50–70 is reasonable); in the *early* fifteenth century it could range from 40–80 MM. The pulse is equal to the semi-breve (whole note), normally transcribed today as a half-note.

Mensural Notation and Note Values
Mensural notation is based on the concepts of *perfection* and *imperfection.*

---

72   Also, frequently chorus singers tapped on the shoulders of singers in front of them as they looked at the large MS in front of them

The meter signature O = Renaissance symbol of oneness, completeness *(there is no end and no beginning)*; 3 symbolized *perfection*—the Christian theology of the Holy Trinity. The breve contains 3 semibreves (whole notes); this whole note contains 2 half notes symbolizing *perfect/imperfect.*

The meter signature C (the incomplete O) symbolized *imperfection*; 2 represented the incomplete *imperfection.* The breve contains 2 semibreves (whole notes); this whole note contains 3 half notes symbolizing *imperfect/perfect.*

In the meter signature ⊙ the breve contains 3 semibreves (whole notes); these whole notes contain 3 half notes, symbolizing *perfect/perfect.*

In the meter signature ℂ the breve contains 2 semibreves (whole notes); these whole notes contain 3 half notes, symbolizing *imperfect/perfect.*

The most common note values are the *longa, breve, semi-breve, minum, semi-minum,* and *fusa,* shown here in mensural notation (left) and modern notation (right):

PROPORTIONS

Dupla (2:1) = 2 semibreves (whole notes) in the time of 1 breve *(alla breve)* are represented by C going to ₵ or ⊘, **or** O going to ₵ or ⊘

Tripla (3:1) = 3 semibreves (whole notes) in the time of 1 semi breve are represented by C going to 3 or C 3 or $\frac{3}{1}$ or C$\frac{3}{1}$, **or** O going to 3 or C 3 or $\frac{3}{1}$

Sesquialtera (3:2) = 3 semibreves (whole notes) in the time of 2 are represented by C going to $\frac{3}{2}$ or C^3 C3 or C$\frac{3}{2}$ or ₵ going to $\frac{3}{2}$ or C$\frac{3}{2}$ **or** O going to $\frac{3}{2}$ or C$\frac{3}{2}$ or O$\frac{3}{2}$.

It is important to keep in mind in looking at the above relationships that good performing editions of Renaissance music normally *halve the original note values.*

Editions today replace mensuration and proportional symbols with modern meters in the following manner:

O and Φ are normally transcribed as $\frac{3}{2}$; sometimes as $\frac{3}{4}$; occasionally as $\frac{3}{1}$ or 3

C and ₵ are normally transcribed as **C** or ₵ or $\frac{4}{4}$ or $\frac{2}{2}$; sometimes $\frac{4}{2}$ or $\frac{2}{4}$ or $\frac{4}{1}$

GENRE AND STYLE EVOLUTION AND THE CHANGING MEANING OF *ALLA BREVE* (₵ OR Φ)

Between 1400 and 1600 the speed of the pulse (*tactus*) tends to slow down; the note values get shorter (i.e., quicker). In the early fifteenth century *alla breve* may be interpreted as twice as fast or considerably faster, especially in the older traditional genres, mass, chanson, lieder.

In very early Mass Kyries of Dufay and Ockeghem the tripartite sections of the Kyrie, Christe, Kyrie are represented by contrasting note values:

Kyrie I = slow long notes

Christe = quicker moving notes

Kyrie II = *alla breve* with quicker notes, then very quick moving notes

These tempo changes heighten the intended emotions: contemplative, personal, urgent plea.

In Dufay, Compère, Senfl, Isaac, Josquin *chanson* and *lieder* the meaning of *alla breve* may be frequently taken as literal; the breve = 80 MM. In fifteenth century early motets of Dufay and Ockeghem the semi-breve tempo seems to range from 68–76 MM; *alla breve* may be meant as "faster."

Motet, the more progressive form, was a catalyst for change; the origin of the word "motet" derives from the French word *mots* ("words"). Especially in the hands of Josquin, words became the guiding impetus for the change in compositional styles reflecting the impact of *humanism.* Word expression began to affect tempo: note values were shorter; pulse began to slow to make room for faster notes; thus, the meaning of *alla breve* began to change. *Alla breve* in Josquin's music means "faster."

By the late sixteenth century C and ₵ became interchangeable *Sesquialtera* (**3:2**) is the most frequent proportion from duple to triple 1400–1600

Tripla (**3:1**) in fifteenth and sixteenth centuries are rare. By the early seventeenth century *tripla* returns. For example, Schütz's motets of his *Geistliche Chormusik* (1648) normally require 3:1 proportions.

A GUIDE TO RENAISSANCE MUSIC EDITIONS TODAY

The best editions normally *halve* the original note values. A responsible editor will differentiate clearly the original composer's notation from changes. *If* the editor has halved the notation, observe the consequences:

- the *semi breve* (whole note) in the original will appear as a half note
- *proportional* signs will relate to half-note relationships: **2:1; 3:1; or 3:2**
- an O mensuration sign is normally written as a $\frac{3}{2}$ meter sign
- C or ₵ are written as **C,** $\frac{2}{2}, \frac{4}{2}$, occasionally $\frac{4}{4}$ in old editions

Written indications of dynamics, phrasing, articulation, or tempo are editorial ideas. Key signatures with sharps or with two or more flats represent editorial transpositions.

Music with quick changes in meter usually reflect an editor's attempt to equate barline stress with syllabic stress; these are not proportional changes. Proportional changes from duple to triple in Renaissance music occur in larger sections, usually denoting a change of text *affect*.

TEMPO: PRACTICAL APPLICATIONS

The speed of the half note (originally whole note) is about 60 MM; 50–70 MM is reasonable. In the *early* fifteenth century to accommodate the ₵ sign, the extremes *may* be 40–80. A $\frac{3}{2}$ meter at the beginning of a piece normally represents the original ○ mensuration sign: the division of the breve into **3** whole notes and division of the whole into **2** half notes. The speed of the half note in ○ mensuration $\left(\frac{3}{2}\right)$ is the same as the speed of the half note in duple $\left(\frac{2}{2} \text{ or } \frac{4}{4}\right)$ normally between 50–70 MM.

There are no barlines in Renaissance music; *feel* the pulse in 2; do not emphasize bar-line stress—there is none! To energize linear forward motion in polyphonic textures, conduct in 4; however, avoid beat accents on 2 and 4.

Rubato is inherent in Renaissance music, especially apparent in the ebb and flow of polyphonic textures and at cadences. Do not place the music in a straitjacket. Allow subtle tempo changes at the ends of phrases in Gregorian chant; "the idea of retarding at cadences seems to have been transmitted (from Gregorian chant) also to polyphonic music"[73]

---

73   Hudson, ibid, p. 7

The size of the ensemble coupled with the room acoustics will affect the actual speed of the *tactus* (pulse).

In making decisions about proportional change, 3 to 1, or 3 to 2, study the text. An uplifting duple (ca. 62–68 MM) often is paired with a stately triple with a serene text—a $\frac{3}{2}$ proportion (3 half notes in the time of 2). An example is Josquin's "Ave Maria...Virgo serena." Also, texts of festive duple and stately triple may be $\frac{3}{2}$. Contemplative duple and joyful triple may be $\frac{3}{1}$.

In the sixteenth century, $\frac{3}{1}$ proportions are rare. Victoria's "O magnum mysterium" seems to be an exception. In this case, a contemplative serious text in *duple* contrasts with words of exultation in triple. The half-note duple pulse (ca. 50) is complemented with 3 half-notes of triple; thus, 3 half-notes are equal to one half-note (ca. 50 MM).

By the early seventeenth century composers began to use more frequently the *tripla* 3:1 proportion. As mentioned above, Heinrich Schütz's motets of *Geistliche Chormusik* illustrate 3:1 proportions throughout this marvelous collection.

PHRASING

Mensuration and proportion symbols, chant-groups, hemiolas, textures, text

Mensuration signs O and C inherently group notes together:

O = 3 whole notes in a breve with 2 half notes in a whole note

C = 2 whole notes in a breve and 2 half notes in a whole note.

Subtle micro-phrasing is inherently implied by these note-groups. Most modern editions halve these note values. In modern editions O is written normally as $\frac{3}{2}$; C is written as C, $\frac{2}{2}$, $\frac{4}{2}$ or $\frac{4}{4}$.

In Renaissance music, metrical proportions between duple sections that are followed by triple meter sections require adjustments in phrase-groupings (macro and micro) because of the inherent change of note values.

Renaissance polyphonic lines are based on chant. Each melodic line is asymmetrical. Phrase independent lines in groups of 3 or 2 (quarter notes in modern editions).

Hemiolas occur in triple meters: a) at cadences; b) within individual polyphonic lines; and c) frequently in homophonic textures when vertical phrasing governs the strong/weak syllabification of the text. Composers consistently employ hemiolas to highlight text as well as to signal the close of a section, especially a final cadence; hemiolas become a built-in ritard. Hemiolas are a composer's expressive rhythmic nuance, and require considerable dynamic attention by using ⟨ ⟩.

Textural changes inherently affect phrasing: polyphonic/homophonic; syllabic/melismatic; open/closed; polyrhythmic/homo-rhythmic.

In polyphonic textures, chant note-groups take priority over syllabic stress; in homophony, syllabic stress takes precedence.

PHRASING: PRACTICAL APPLICATIONS

Inherent in phrasing Renaissance polyphonic lines is expression: *subtle* dynamic nuance wedded with *rubato*. It is the asymmetry of the lines—the fact that there is no regular continuous flow, but a subtle irregularity within the flow—that creates this intrinsic expression.

The origins of *chant phrasing* are derived from notation which can be traced back to the early ninth century when symbols were written above texts, reminders to singers of how a chant melody was sung. By the early twelfth century neumatic notation and a 4-line staff developed, indicating notes often visually connected with ligatures in 2- to 5-note groups, forming symmetric or asymmetric patterns. These symmetric/asymmetric patterns cause linear flow to have irregular micro phrase-groups.

When four overlapping vocal parts sing polyphony the expression of each line is best telegraphed by mimicking these irregularities, modestly highlighting them with subtle phrasing, dynamics and rubato. In a triple note-group crescendo *subtly* from beat 3 to 1; beat 2 is weaker. The subtle crescendo activates forward motion; the subtle relaxation in triple note-groups after beat 1 creates a subtle momentary diminuendo. These suggestions will highlight, differentiate, and project the inherent supple and subtle dynamic undulation of polyphony.

Maintaining and projecting expressive nuances in a contrapuntal fabric of multiple voices is challenging but stunningly rewarding. Dynamically enhanced phrasing (as described above) may be the *most* expressive value to be sought in Renaissance choral performance.

Composers used *homorhythmic textures* to emphasize text. Phrase and articulate strong/weak syllables with subtle dynamic stresses ⊂⊃ within this texture.

Hemiolas are inherently expressive; they are meant to highlight the approach of a cadence; if they occur within a phrase they usually stress text syllabification.

Dynamics

Line/Phrase Balance; Changes in Harmony, Melody, Rhythm, or Texture
Sing polyphonic lines by expressively shaping and differentiating symmetric/asymmetric note-groups. Achieve balance by requiring

dynamic change, re-voicings, and/or transposition. To achieve SATB balance in homophony, reinforce with dynamics. Renaissance choral music may be viewed as consort music—4 SATB viols, sackbuts, recorders—with vocal "instruments" that create sound in the same way. Balance the SATB parts.

Much of Renaissance choral music written for the soprano fits the range of the modern mezzo; the alto that of a first tenor; and the tenor a bari-tenor range. Reinforce these ranges to balance the ensemble. Some alto parts are quite low. Reinforce altos with baritones or tenors to help balance the inherent equal-voice textures.

Long held notes can obscure fast moving parts. Allow them to be heard by singing long notes more softly.

PRACTICAL APPLICATION OF DYNAMICS

Practical application of dynamics relates to *changes* in harmony, melody, rhythm, and texture. Each of these elements requires awareness of expressive potential and attention in rehearsal techniques and goals.

Change in Harmony

Renaissance composers were aware of harmony as a means of projecting *text affect* or the direct expression of word painting. Dissonance, chromaticism, chord progressions, and intervallic relationships require subtle expressive crescendos and diminuendos.

When a composer adds a sharp or a flat in the context of a chord, this draws attention to the word. Highlight chromatic change with subtle *dynamic stress.*

Chord progressions[74] suggest *dynamic nuance:* IV–I suggests a diminuendo; V–I suggests a crescendo/resolve; major followed

---

74 A full explanation of the relationship of dynamic nuance to vertical and horizontal intervals appears in Chapter 15.

by minor chords imply diminuendo; changes from minor to major modes may imply crescendo.

Change in Melody

Melodic contours, ranges, tessituras, and note-groups call for subtle dynamic nuances. The intervallic relationships among vocal parts and structural elements related to the primary melody versus a filler held note or a pedal function all require attention to the primary musical line.

Rising and falling melodic lines may call for a crescendo (for the rising contour) and diminuendo (for the falling contour).

Structurally important low notes require dynamic reinforcement; long note at ends of phrases especially in high ranges, need to be sung softer to make audible the primary melodic line; guard against long notes covering moving parts.

Singing *cantus firmus* lines require care. When this long-note line moves to another, crescendo slightly into the new long note, stressing it slightly. In polyphonic textures, this allows a *cantus firmus* to be heard, but it can subtly recede slightly into the background to allow the quick moving polyphonic lines to clearly be heard.

Long held notes obscure faster moving notes. Highlight quick-moving parts with stronger dynamics and subtle vocal articulation.

Change in Rhythm

Change in rhythm is affected by change in mensuration, proportion, note-groups, hemiolas, sustained notes vs. quick-moving parts, and text underlay. Renaissance composers wrote expressive nuances that directly effect change in tempo transmitted by changes in mensuration and proportion signs.

Proportional signs are a highly expressive nuance in the Renaissance and require *dynamic differentiation*. Note values increase in speed by

2:1, 3:2, and **3:1** proportions. Speed affects quick notes; the faster notes require sharper articulation, especially in imitative textures. Fast notes typically highlight verbs of action and emotion in the Renaissance.

In homophonic textures, the strong/weak syllabification is enhanced by emphasizing natural word stress.

Hemiolas act as a *rhythmic brake*, a nuance that highlights a cadence, drawing out two groups of three beats by re-phrasing them into three groups of two.

Change in Texture

Much Renaissance music is imitative. Crescendos occur naturally as vocal parts accumulate, especially when the sequence of entrances is from lower to higher voices.

The more voice parts the fuller the sound. Each entrance must be clearly heard. After the initial entrances soften to allow the next entrances to be heard.

Low ranges require dynamic support. If the melodic line is structurally important, provide *dynamic projection and articulation*.

Polyphonic textures necessitate considerable nuance: the rise and fall of melodic lines, the range and tessitura of vocal parts, the natural, ever-shifting shades of dynamics derived from groups of twos and threes, and the inherent dynamic vitality that is felt in the ebb and flow of independently phrased polyphonic lines.

In homorhythmic textures, all parts speak as one. Interest is focused on the text; word stress becomes the primary concern, rather than the interplay of independent lines. Higher-pitched homophonic passages will sound louder than lower-pitched one, and open textures clearer than closed or dense textures. Introduce shifts of dynamic weight and/or re-voicing to realize the composer's intention of having all parts speak as one.

In homophonic textures, tuning, balance, clear diction, and expressive syllabic stress require dynamic attention. If a vocal part is too low for singers, re-voice the passage.

Head motifs of polyphonic compositions must be heard. Punching out entrances is just as abhorrent to the style as employing a continuous hushed pianissimo, as if this will reflect "holiness" in a sacred work. The interplay between head motifs and quick moving vocal parts requires attention and adjustment with dynamics that clarify the vocal texture in polyphonic structures.

Hexachords, Solmization, and Modes: More Details for the Interested Reader

In Renaissance theory there were three hexachords (sets of six specific pitches). All singers read their vocal part with solmization syllables, using two hexachords—based on C or G, or based on C and F if B was in the key signature.

Singers' solmization syllables:	ut re mi fa sol la
On C ("natural" hexachord)	c d e f g a
On G ("hard" hexachord)	g a b c d e
On F (with B♭ in signature; "soft" hexachord)	f g a B♭ c d

This famous phrase describes a rule for when to use *musica ficta* (i.e., usually altering the pitch with an accidental): "Una nota super la semper est canendum fa": "A note above "la" is always understood as "fa."

For example, in the C hexachord, if the melody goes one note above *la* and back to *la,* the note above *la* is sung as *fa*; this created a *mi-fa* half-step relationship that changes that note to a B♭. A *fa* between two *sols* becomes *mi,* creating the half-step relationship, G–F♯–G. A *sol* between two *las becomes* a *mi* (e.g., a G between two a's becomes g♯)

Singers mentally moved from the C hexachord to the G hexachord if the range of their part was greater than a 6th. If the key signature had one flat, singers moved from the F hexachord to the C hexachord if the range of their part was greater than a 6th.

Modes

Modes often are revealed by the melodic outline and range of the tenor part and the descending note to the *finalis* of the mode, at cadences. The primary modes are:

- Dorian (D–d) contains the sadness of *d, e, f* (minor), and the joy of *g, a, b* (major); thus *dorian* is a "mixed mode"; it sounds rather serious, thoughtful.
- Phrygian (E–e) has a very distinct sound, created by the half-step descending from *f* to *e* that sounds sad, mournful, imploring.
- Lydian (F–f) is arresting; play *f* scales over and over without B♭. It feels entirely unresolved; a sense of other worldliness; exotic filled, with tension, even quasi-erotic.
- Mixolydian (G-g) is a much "happier" sounding mode.

Modes	Name	Range	Finalis	Common Cadential Notes
I	Dorian	D–d	D	D, A, F, g, c
II	Hypodorian	a–A	D	D, A, F, g, c
III	Phrygian	E–e	E	E, A, C, g, f
IV	Hypophrygian	b–B	E	E, A, C, g, f
V	Lydian	F–f	F	F, C, A, d, g
VI	Hypolydian	c–C	F	F, A, B , d, g
VII	Mixolydian	G–g	G	G, D, C, f, a
VIII	Hypomixolydian	d–D	G	G, D, f, a

While the mode is usually determined by the Tenor voice descending to the *finalis at the final cadence*, sometimes the "tenor" is in another part! (The word *tenor* is derived from the Italian word *tenere*— to hold; it was the part that normally *holds* the mode.) If there is a flat in the key signature the mode is transposed up a 4th. If there is a sharp in the key signature the original had one flat.

CHAPTER 14

SINGING POLYPHONY TODAY ∼

WHERE HAVE ALL THE FLOWERS GONE?
HISTORICAL OVERVIEW

In the beginning, first came melody (chant), then many melodies (*poly phony*). Harmony was a by-product of simultaneous independent melodies, creating chords of three or four notes. The harmony produced was suspended between well-crafted vocal lines. Words inspired composers to compose. Throughout history, composers expressed text through change in harmony, melody, rhythm, and texture by creating a rich vocabulary of expression, a mellifluous balance of homophony and polyphony. Special texts required vertical textures to directly serve the text and allow listeners to clearly hear the words.

In current choral culture *homophony* is the norm, and composers recognizing this trend compose vertical music; publishers follow suit. Are singers, conductors, composers, and publishers no longer interested in polyphony? Has singing polyphony become too hard? Are singers no longer experiencing melodically and rhythmically independent lines? Are conductors afraid to break the homophonic security of easy access learning?

In attending choral concerts of the American Choral Directors Association, beginning in 1967, the IMC 1978, NCCO 2006, and Chorus America 2014, I have observed that performances of polyphonic music from the past *six* centuries is increasingly rare. At regional and national conferences one primarily hears new music composed of vertical sonorities. Verticality appears to reign over polyphony. Do composers think choral singers are intimidated by polyphony? Have publishers decided only homophony will sell? Why do we rarely hear Renaissance masterpieces? Are conductors intimidated by specialists who espouse informed performance?

Polyphonic works composed three centuries before Bach are rarely performed. The result is that generations of students have only a limited view of the rich range of styles and genres from 1400–1700. Students have little insight into the performing practices of these eras, and now lack the musicianship required to sing polyphonic gems and masterworks by Johannes Ockeghem (c. 1410–1497) to Heinrich Schütz (1615–1672). Why? Could it be because, for the past forty-five years, we have been strongly influenced by recordings of early music ensembles that espouse informed performance?

Conductors, and Choirs Today

Today, conductors are concerned about performing early music with comparatively large high school, college, community, and church choirs; they ask, "how can my choir sound like these ensembles that espouse informed performance?" Are we intimidated? Are we afraid to be *wrong?* I think we are, but I don't think we should be! The question we should ask is, "how can we use our stylistic and analytical insights in an informed way to bring polyphony alive, today, regardless of the size of our ensembles?"

Do choirs have to sound like the Tallis Scholars? No! Is *that* how Palestrina's choirs sounded? No! Can I perform Bach's *St. Matthew Passion* with my 75-voice Concert Choir? Yes! Can my chamber choir of thirty-five singers perform Monteverdi madrigals written for the virtuoso soloists of the Italian courts? Yes! Can I perform Haydn's *Lord Nelson Mass* with my 250-voice community choir? Yes! We can and we must, or face losing the Western choral heritage.

In *Early Music America* in an article by Vicente Charvarria entitled "Singing Polyphony in the Twenty-first Century" (May 2017), a conversation occurs among five professional musicians who recently formed a Miami-based ensemble. None of the musicians had any experience singing polyphony. They came from diverse musical backgrounds. Two are professional singers, pianists, and active church musicians. One is a high school choir director, composer and organist; one a college faculty member, and one a conductor and musicologist. Following is a synopsis of the article.

EMA Moderator: As modern musicians approaching music that's 500 years old, what is the single biggest challenge you've faced in approaching polyphony?

JM: I think there's a more horizontal way we need to think, and I think as musicians today when we sing in a 'choral' kind of way, we're thinking in a very vertical way. I need to adjust [my thinking] . . . this is more fluid; you're listening to line. It's a different feel, a different way of listening. These singer-composers who worked 500 years ago, they lived and breathed this musical language from a very early age until adulthood. They wrote how they knew was the way to write, much the way we do today, except we're trained very specifically in our harmonic language (whether tonal or post-tonal). We're trained in a rather rigid idea of what harmony should be. We write that way, we perform that way, we sing that way; whereas here, in essence, we're trying to recreate something that works in a different language.

EMA Moderator: What has attracted you to polyphony?

JM: I think what's drawn me to polyphony is going back in time, something we've not really been accustomed to in our current, modern choral world as we think of it. Every line is independent. That's unique. Every line stands alone. And the relationship is so different! Our relationship singing-wise is completely different. One thing I adore is not just the sound but the logic as well. Once you understand how two lines work, what's happening between them . . . it doesn't detract but rather increases the artistic value, just knowing that there's a highly calculated way that two lines work with each other. Once that clicks and makes sense, (a) it becomes a lot easier, but (b) you also appreciate the craftsmanship of these composers.[75]

It was gratifying to read how these professional musicians viewed their "entry points" into the rich and challenging musical rewards of singing polyphony. Their experience directly contrasts with information that appeared in the May 2017 issue of the ACDA *Choral Journal.* Robert J. Ward and Leila Heil wrote an informed article that offers statistically accurate documentation of choral

---

75   ibid., *Early Music America* May 2017

works performed at national conventions of the American Choral Directors Association.[76]

ACDA is an organization established in 1959 with 111 conductors. By 2017, ACDA's membership had grown to more than 20,000 conductors. The core of Ward's and Heil's study divides the styles and genres presented by ACDA choirs into twelve categories: the numbers and percentages of repertoire performed are listed in ten-year periods from 1961 to 2017. The results are stunning, though not surprising. For example, from 1990–1999, out of 771 pieces performed, 56 were from the Renaissance; among the 1,209 choral works performed during 2000–2010, 83 were from the Renaissance, or 6.86 percent.

CONFIRMING CONCERN

My fifty-year observations of ACDA Conferences from 1967 to 2017 confirm Ward's and Heil's research: there has been a decrease in the performance of Renaissance choral music from the 1960s to the present. As the authors point out, of all compositions performed, "choral repertoire from the Medieval through the Romantic eras consists of 26 percent of the whole; Ethnic/Multicultural, Folk Songs, Spirituals/Gospel, Hymns/Carols 23 percent; modern composers (categorized by "early" and late") total 51 percent of the whole!" I would add, 90 percent of the compositions written between 1975–2015 are primarily homophonic.

Ward and Heil confirm my greatest concern: "statistics of this survey indicate that the younger generation is not getting the message that performing the earlier repertoire is standard fare and

---

76   *Choral Journal*, May 2017, pp. 37–42. Robert Ward is Director of Choral Activities, The Ohio State University; Leila Heil is Assistant Professor of Choral Music Education, University of Colorado.

integral to both understanding the most basic element of choral music (polyphony) and advancement in the profession. ACDA conferences today, 'whether they intend to or not,' project the idea that 'earlier repertoire is out of vogue' and contrary to advancement and recognition in the American choral academy."[77]

Compositions of unrelieved homophony diminish the chance for students to experience singing their own separate parts. The singers are robbed of experiencing the melodic, rhythmic, and expressive independence of their vocal line. The by-product of polyphony is that it shapes and challenges the musicianship of singers. When rhythms and melodies are separated from one another, choral singers are freed from the relentless experience of harmonizing the principal melody.

As William Dehning poignantly writes in a "Letter to the Editor" of the November 2010 issue of the ACDA *Choral Journal*, "Programming music of the past that others might know could be viewed as a risk, because they might not agree with our interpretation . . . Truth be told, I think this is the real reason some choose not to perform a Brahms motet at a convention. We're simply scared silly to put something up there that many may know, and not because we think that choral musicians are tired of hearing it."[78]

New Thoughts

This topic has been my concern for more than two generations of students; what follows are my thoughts about how and why we have reached this current choral conundrum. I believe many choral conductors today have been reliving the educational premises and values of their predecessors. In the 1970s, when CDs of "informed

---

77   Ibid, Ward and Heil, ACDA *Choral Journal*, May 2017

78   William Dehning, "Letter to the Editor" *Choral Journal* 51 no. 4 (November 2010); pg. 8

performance practice" with professional chamber choirs were in full swing, many conductors began to lose confidence in performing Renaissance music "in the way it should be done." As knowledge of performance practices grew, conductors felt ill-at-ease with those practices, especially from 1400–1640. Choral conducting students of the 1990s, the next generation, many mirroring the inclinations of their choir directors and teachers, began to feel unprepared for the performance of early music. By today, this fact undermined their desire to perform polyphony especially with big choirs. The result was "my big choirs should not (cannot) perform polyphony." If a choir and its conductor want to sing polyphony, questions arose: "how can I get my choir to sound like that? How can I make each melodic line so expressive? Will my big choir ever be able to perform polyphony in a correct way?" The answer is a resounding Yes!

Ward and Heil confirm this affirmation, "an understanding of historical performance practices should be a freeing element. Scholarship gives us license to be creative and to use our modern resources in a way that breathes new life and vitality into a music that deserves to be more than just historical documents on library shelves."[79] Dehning adds, "We are educators hoping to educate our students, our colleagues, our selves. And none of us has the definitive answer to anything."[80]

Over my professional career I have conducted large choirs, mixed, men's, and women's choirs.[81] Throughout these years my choirs were filled with liberal arts undergraduate students; we performed choral literature from the fifteenth to the twenty-first centuries,

---

79 Ibid, Ward and Heil

80 William Dehning, "Broadside," *Choral Journal* 38, no. 5 (December 1997): pp. 25–26

81 1967–'68 the Men's Glee Club at Lehigh University; 1969–1978, the Women's and Mixed Choirs at Vassar College; for 32 years at Harvard University, the Harvard Glee Club, Radcliffe Choral Society, and HR Collegium Musicum.

both polyphonic and homophonic, sacred and secular, a cappella and choral-instrumental masterworks from Monteverdi's *Vespers of 1610* to Paul Moravec's *Songs of Love and War* (2004).

I have consistently performed a cappella repertoire with choirs of 60–70 voices, and major works from Haydn's masses to twentieth-century repertoire with 185 voices. Polyphonic and contrapuntal textures comprise much of this repertoire. I know from experience that polyphony by Ockeghem, Schütz, Brahms, and of the twenty-first century can be performed at a high level with undergraduate, mostly non-music major choirs.

My desire is to be an important voice to urge conductors to program polyphony in order to develop independence, style, and musicianship with singers of all ages, all educational levels, and in choirs large and small. In concluding this chapter on singing polyphony today, here are thoughts and materials I have used at various workshops and lecture demonstrations. [82]

BRING BACK THE FLOWERS TODAY: SUMMARY AND AFFIRMATION OF FAITH

Today we hear two trends: (1) concerts that offer only a glimpse of the choral genres of the past six centuries which are rich in polyphony and counterpoint; and (2) composers confirming their principal means of expression as best served through harmonic lushness and dynamic contrast in a texture of unrelieved homophony. Both trends diminish the chance for students to be challenged by singing melodic and rhythmic lines unhinged from each other, offering each part a larger range of independent expression.

---

82   ACDA National Conference in Dallas, 2013, the IMC 2014 National Seminar at Rutgers University, and the Chorus America National Conference in Los Angeles, in 2017.

Imagine the improvement of the choir when each part learns to maintain rhythmic and melodic independence. Imagine the relief of an alto liberated from harmonic filler parts as she becomes an equal partner with her S, T, B colleagues. In homophonic textures sopranos most often sing the high main melody In polyphonic textures imagine how liberated the sopranos might feel imitating the melody initiated by the bass part, or serving as an important harmonic filler in an SATB contrapuntal texture. Tenors no longer have to be the sopranos' duet partner. Imagine basses liberated from the root of chords, enjoying the independence of their own melody unhinged from the SAT parts and being able to sing their line expressively! Singing polyphony develops self-confidence, independence, style, and musicianship. This is *music education*!

At the ACDA National Conference in Dallas in 2013 I presented an interest session with the Texas Tech Concert Choir (under the direction of Richard Bjella) in which I sought to cut through the current choral conundrum by demonstrating rehearsal techniques for large choirs wanting to sing polyphony.[83] The interest session was a catalyst for conductors who wanted to perform polyphony but had not done so. I rehearsed brief excerpts from three contrasting motets: Ockeghem's "Alma redemptoris Mater," Palestrina's "Sicut cervus desiderat," and Brahms's "Warum ist das Licht gegeben." By differentiating the inherent expressive nuances of the melodic and rhythmic contours of each polyphonic line, with specific rehearsal techniques we illustrated how SATB singers can expressively and

---

83 Similarly, and with equal distinction, I was assisted at my lecture/demonstration at the Intercollegiate National Seminar at Rutgers University with the excellent assistance of the Men's Glee Club from Penn State University, Christopher Kiver, conductor, and at the Chorus America National Conference in LA with an excellent choral ensemble chosen from the Angeles Chorale by their conductor John Sutton. For both occasions, I offered as demonstration examples my editions (for men and mixed choirs) of Palestrina's "Sicut cervus." The educational results I describe above were equally (and vociferously) appreciated by very varied audiences of conductors.

independently complement each other. The goal of my presentation was to stimulate confidence in singing choral polyphony of a range of styles and eras with choirs of varied sizes

I placed the Texas Tech Concert Choir in mixed positions. Singing in mixed positions enhances the responsibility of individual singers, and provides an opportunity to develop self-reliance, independence, and musicianship. The results: singers develop good ears, independent rhythm, and pride in their ability to get their own part right. Reinforcing correct notes and rhythms, and especially singing the expressive gestures of their own part, rests squarely on the shoulder of each member of the choir. Encouraging conductors to relish the experience of performing polyphony with large choirs, where each part is responsible for independent music-making, manifests personal, educational, and musical rewards, inspired by the polyphonic process.

At the conclusion of this interest session, and also with my own choirs at Harvard and with many amateur choral singers, I have asked, "why perform polyphony today?" Below are some of their responses.

1. **I love to sing polyphony**
    Each musician is responsible for holding his own part while remaining closely attuned to the other lines. Polyphony is the perfect music for me. It always makes me happiest to be making music with others, each of us responsible for carrying our own part while being exquisitely aware and responsive to the others.

2. **A metaphor for human understanding**
    I find working with adults in particular that singing polyphony can act as a metaphor for human

understanding—harmony in the spiritual rather than musical sense. These are people who bring a deep understanding of our mutual condition into the room, and who love and thrive from being able to "exercise those muscles." "E pluribus unum"— from many, one—unity through independently supporting each other—knowing when to take turns.

3. **Singing with "too big" choruses** (professional choral conductor)

   While most singers associate polyphony with music since Bach it is clear that the lessons we learn from singing and teaching Josquin, Byrd, Tallis, Palestrina, Gibbons, Victoria and even earlier are essential to an informed view of choral music after 1700. I work with a large volunteer adult chorus of about 140 singers; we have taken on many polyphonic works. Most recently and successfully to audience and singers' acclaim: Byrd: *Mass for Four Voices*, incredibly accessible and one of the best experiences I've had; other works: masses and motets of Palestrina and Victoria; concerted works of Schütz and Gabrieli.

4. **Singing polyphony enlarges our understanding of Western music**

   For an adult chorus or a collegiate or secondary school chorus, teaching the great works of polyphony adds centuries to their understanding of Western music. Because the piano is the entry point for *so* many musicians (myself included), we all start out with a stunted view of history— i.e., Bach and beyond. And that's all wonderful, except that there are a good three centuries of published music that go before the three centuries we are most familiar with.

Polyphony aids in a mastery of all musical styles. The connection to the great age of the fugue is easy to grasp—shaping the independent vocal line, learning to listen and find your place in the texture, etc. Teaching active listening, polyphony also helps tune the chords when we sing in homophonic textures. A choir that learns to sing polyphony well will not simply park itself on the cadence, but will continue to think, listen, and tune actively.

5. **Polyphony offers independence and awareness**
    Performing pitches and rhythm correctly, but also creating individual gesture and line within. We acquire an awareness of function in polyphony that leads to better awareness of function in singing homophonic music. Performing polyphony in mixed positions compounds the benefits—performing independently reinforces the goal of the academy to produce independent thinkers.

6. **Polyphonic music offers singers a challenge and an opportunity**
    It challenges them to know their own part well, to emphasize its important passages, and to de-emphasize its less important parts. It gives them an opportunity to weave together a rich tapestry of sound and more importantly, rehearsing polyphony teaches singers to rely upon one another, to build on each other's strengths, and to unite as a group through hearing their own part both separate from yet united with the other parts.

7. **Polyphony and homophony**
    Having sung with a wonderful ensemble that performed chant for years, I find this topic [polyphony/homophony] particularly interesting. I had to think a lot about the value

and beauty of homophonic music when I was singing it, having all my life kind of taken for granted that beautiful music was polyphonic. I got there, but it took a while.

8. **The first time I ever saw the Harvard Glee Club perform** I was entranced by the swaying of its members as they sang Renaissance polyphony. There was such an organic sense of motion in the music that it seemed to be infecting the singers, whose bodies manifested the cascading lines. I don't believe I had ever heard polyphony before that point, but I was immediately and forever after captivated by the beauty of how lines of music can be traded off from part to part in a cyclical, building style that made the music seem alive. I know next to nothing about music theory, but polyphony is what initially intrigued me to audition for the Glee Club, a decision that has enriched and continues to enrich my life in countless ways.

9. **I like singing polyphony for several reasons** Each part provides an opportunity for individual expression which is more satisfying as a singer. I enjoy the variation in lines, harmonies and effects. With an expert composer like Josquin or Palestrina you can really appreciate the genius and the special moments from the "inside."

10. **I'm trying to teach the idea that vocal polyphony represents a conversation.** (conductor of a high school chorus) Singing homophony is fun and easy, two sure ingredients towards success in human beings; but individualism is another. People tend to see polyphony as complicated but it should I think be simply furthering an initial point and in the end giving voice to more individuals and ideas.

From my own experience, the shape of Renaissance melodic lines, born out of Gregorian chant, develops independence in three forms: melodic, rhythmic, and expressive. Over time, this simultaneous sound-continuum produces a mesmerizing, quasi-ethereal, neither-here-nor-there feeling. These inherent emotions are amplified by the expressive power of the modes. The result: choral singers, conductors, and listeners frequently experience *euphoria,* and moments of transcendence.

Through my many years of experience conducting amateur singers, it has been clear that a cappella gems from the fifteenth through the twenty-first centuries, and choral-orchestral works from Monteverdi and Schütz to Stravinsky and Britten, challenge and reward each singer. Rehearsing and performing polyphony energizes the development of musicianship, self-confidence, and independence, as well as vocal development in supporting their own line. At the same time, singers are educating themselves to the inherent expressive values of past eras, styles, and genres, thereby developing a rich perspective about the history of choral music.

CHAPTER 15

THE EXPRESSIVE POWER OF INTERVALS ⁓

Musical meaning is the catalyst for music making. Both vertical and horizontal intervals possess a rich vocabulary of meaning. Chords and melodies create ever-changing expressive meanings, suggestions, expectations, questions, confirmations. Intervals are the aural channels through which expressive nuances are projected. Vertical and horizontal intervals generate emotional responses, a phenomenon not always noticed. Conductors and performers often fail to recognize the emotional connections of varied patterns of harmonic and melodic intervals.

The theme of this book can be summed up in two words: emotional connection. The history of western choral music is based upon the intertwining relationships of intervals, creating a palate of sound, a mosaic of *affetti* filled with emotional undercurrents. As Don Campbell says in his important book, *Music: Physician for Times to Come*, "Music moves. Not only emotionally, but bodily: music dances inwardly, and incites to gesture, to dance, outwardly.

Song and gesture both contain movement generated by the musical thought and form. . . even thinking music, without sound, involves the experience of movement in imagination."[84]

The earliest notational symbols of chant did not represent notes nor rhythms but were written symbols of nuances. These symbols were to remind singers of the melodies as well as inherent expressive nuances developed through eight centuries of aural tradition. The melodies were meant to adorn the sacred texts. The early symbols placed above the texts were related entirely to expressive nuances that would project feelings.

Connecting the composer's emotional sound picture to understand and highlight a score, conductors must find the handles of creativity implied by the composer's notation. These handles are catalysts to inspire a conductor's creative imagination.

What are meaningful handles? How are they determined? The answer seems simple, though frequently only felt subconsciously. In my long experience, I have tried to make *conscious* stimuli that tug at my emotions. At first I felt them keenly through studying and performing Renaissance music. I realized my handles were connected to insights that led me to understand these basic concepts: *perfection* and *naturalness,* and *the expressive power of intervals.*

Horizontal Intervals

Historically, the development of melodic contours and intervallic relationships in Gregorian chant became the basis for Renaissance polyphony. Chant, medieval, and Renaissance music share a common spirit; their melodies reflect varied ranges and intervallic relationships labeled by Greeks as *modes.* Each had an associated *plagal mode* called *hypo,* a scale of the same intervallic relationship though starting

---

84   Don Campbell, *Music: Physician for Times to Come,* Quest Books, 2006, 124

a fourth below. Our major and minor modes are derived from Greek hypo modes: Hypolydian (C to C), and Hypodorian (a to a).[85]

As noted in a previous chapter, major and minor modes frequently serve as expressions of the *affects,* such as happy or sad. Renaissance composers portrayed the mood of the texts through the use of modes. Dorian D-d) sounds serious, taming passions; Phrygian (E-e) sounds sad, sometimes exotic, vehement; Lydian (F-f) passionate, strong, quasi erotic; Mixolydian (G-g) sounds happy, playful, serene. We can feel these moods by playing these scales both ascending and descending on the white notes of a piano. Why? Because of the whole and half step sequences.[86]

As Aniruddh Patel describes in *Music, Language, and the Brain,* "Musical melody is more than a mere succession of pitches: it is a network of interconnected patterns in the mind *derived* from a sequence of pitch variation. That is, the human perceptual system converts a two-dimensional sequence (pitch vs. time) into a rich set of perceived relationships."[87]

We all remember melodies we sang during childhood years; we can still recall many by heart. From the popular songs of the Beatles, to Christmas carols, folk songs, patriotic songs, and church hymns, they stick with us creating feelings and moods. We experience meaningful nostalgia when we sing or hear them.

Melodies vary enormously: linear scales, melodic leaps, ascending, descending, short, long, and combinations of multiple relationships. Playing melodies of varied types is an exploration

---

85 Dorian mode is based on the scale D to D; Hypodorian is based on the scale A to A (our Aeolian or minor mode); for both, the *finalis* is on D; Mixolydian is based on a scale from G to G; Hypomixolydian is based on the scale from C to C (our Ionian or major mode); for both, the *finalis* is on C.

86 Dorian: w h w w w h w; Phrygian: h w w w h w w; Lydian: w w w h w w h; Mixolydian: w h w w h w.

87 Aniruddh D. Patel, *Music, Language, and the Brain,* 190

worth experiencing.[88] Each elicits an emotion. Play varied short-note melodies (three to five notes) and see how they affect you. Do the same with longer melodies. The experience elicits *feelings* inherent in the innumerable combinations and sequences of note patterns.

VERTICAL INTERVALS

From earliest times, expressions of mood and emotion were related to intervallic symbols of perfection and naturalness. Reinforced by reverberant cathedrals, perfect intervals corresponded to the natural overtone series. In medieval vocal polyphony, pure intervallic ratios were related to theology: unison 1:1 (God); octave 2:1 (God/Father); and fifth 3:2 (God, Father, Son). These mathematical ratios were the vertical intervals used at cadences.

By the middle of the Renaissance (c. 1520) the interval of the major 3rd (5:4) was found in compositions, though rarely at final cadences. The pure overtone major third (for example e produced by the fundamental C), is out of tune and irreconcilable with the e produced by a series of four pure perfect fifths (C–G–D–A–E). The difference between the two is easily heard; it is not subtle. The lovely sound of a pure major third was especially favored in English fifteenth century sacred music. By the mid-sixteenth century, composers included major thirds in final cadences. This change in compositional attitude necessitated a new tuning system, mean-tone tuning. Mean-tone (or Just Intonation) produces "natural" pure major thirds that are low compared to equal (piano) temperament. Minor thirds were rarely allowed at cadences.

Natural pure intervals infiltrated Renaissance compositions and created the nomenclature of perfect and imperfect intervals.

---

88 Seek short and long melodies of diverse kinds; play each through a few times and write down what you are feeling.

Unisons/octaves, 5ths/4ths are "perfect"; major 3rds/minor 6ths are "imperfect"— they sound "at rest" in the overtone series, and there is no natural tension.[89] Other intervals sound imperfect and call for resolution. We hear them as dissonant: minor and major 2nds, major and minor 7ths; augmented and diminished 4ths and 5ths. Minor 3rds and major 6ths are also imperfect. They have tension and require resolution. Composers signaled a cadence by using the imperfect minor 3rd to contract to a perfect unison, or the imperfect major 6th to expand to the perfect octave at the cadence. To express extreme emotions, such as pain, loss, passion, bitterness, or sadness the exquisite dissonant major 7th or minor 2nd were used, and demanded resolution.

Cadences clarified the structure of music and were used at the conclusion of a segment of text. Renaissance cadences occur on the *finalis* of the mode (D, Dorian; E, Phrygian; F, Lydian; and G, Mixolydian). The major 6th or minor 3rd cadence on the *finalis* occurs *naturally* in both the Phrygian mode (F–D to E) and Lydian (G–E to F); they are built in; however, to cadence on the *finalis* of the Dorian (D) or Mixolydian (G) mode, the major 6th or minor 3rd is not built in. These cadences required a Renaissance performer to sing *musica ficta (false music)* The Dorian mode required a C♯ and E, the Mixolydian required an F♯ and A to create the cadence. One cadential structure used a descending half step to form the cadence (Phrygian

---

89   Teach choirs to tune to the overtone series, especially the major 3rd that in the overtone
      series is quite audibly low compared to the pitch of piano tempered tuning. For
      example, strongly strike and briefly hold a low note (e.g., C two octaves below middle,
      or G a fifth above the low C on the piano; listen for note vibrations. Most clear will be
      the octave and depending upon the acoustics of the room and the position of the piano
      (lift lid up) you will hear the 5th and 3rd; ask singers to cup ears; some acoustics project
      either the 5th or 3rd more loudly; repeat low note several times; ask the basses to sing *in
      unison with a pure vowel* ah or oh, the low note (G); they will produce the same clear
      overtones. Surround the choir with the basses, cup ears; add S, A, or T on the 5th of the
      chord; cup ears, listen for the 3rd.

(F–D to E)), creating an exceedingly poignant and evocative sound. Frequently, Phrygian cadences occurred within phrases to highlight the *affect* of mourning, sadness, or yearning.[90]

Chord progressions occur on various scale degrees within all modes and keys and have intrinsic expressive qualities that can meaningfully be highlighted through the use of dynamics, ranging from obvious to subtle[91]. Combinations of chord progressions create emotional connections, subtle or obvious. As Aniruddh Patel says in his book *Music, Language, and the Brain*, "central to the experience of tonal music is a listener's sense of tension and resolution as a piece unfolds in time . . . this aspect of music . . . is at the very heart of musical understanding . . . the notion of tension is related to the sense of mobility or openness (i.e., a sense that the music must continue), whereas resolution is associated with repose or rest."[92] The sound of a V–I chord progression expresses tension. Tension inherently invites dynamics: V–I = *crescendo*; *diminuendo* = resolve. Quite commonly, we hear an "Amen" IV–I plagal cadence as anticipation (there is no tension), moving to the resolution; we instinctively feel a *diminuendo* (relaxation).

Dynamic and tempo terms began to appear in the seventeenth century.[93] By the eighteenth century, dynamic markings were present in scores to indicate a musical gesture required a certain dynamic. For example, the written *cresc./dim.* were reminders to performers of the inherent *affect* of chord progression, a fact that remains true today. It

---

90   We hear Phrygian cadences frequently in compositions of the Renaissance Baroque; they often appear with a major 7th dissonant appoggiatura or suspension that highlights it. For example, the conclusion of a Handel slow movement frequently occurs with the resolution landing on the dominant, preparing the cheerful fast movement new major key.

91   In Appendix B we see some examples of how several chord progressions suggest dynamic nuances.

92   Patel, *Music, Language,* 256, 257

93   In Schütz's *Geistliche Chormusik* of 1648 we see one example; Schütz marks *Tarde* near the conclusion of his motet *Ich weiss, dass mein Erlöser lebt,* m. 51.

is important to remind ourselves that ca. 1400–1650, composers did not mark scores because they didn't have to. Only *they* performed their music. They could tell the musicians what they wanted to hear.

CHAPTER 16

FINALE ⟋⟍

The topics of this book are diverse and interconnected. The main theme—the emotional connection—permeates the Conductor's Process in all stages:

1. Choosing repertoire
2. Studying the score
3. Developing the mental-aural image
4. Rehearsing, hearing, and fixing
5. Performing—the choir's chance to present the conductor's mental-aural image of "how the composition goes," clearly learned in rehearsal
6. Teaching in the rehearsal by the conductor who gathers insights from the notational symbols used by the composer
7. Forging informed stylistic interpretation
8. Understanding the *gesture* symbolized by notation
9. Evaluating choral progress by listening
10. Conducting with clarity and expressivity in the concert, and Generating emotional connections through mastering choral ensemble.

My special interest in performing Renaissance choral music has heightened my awareness of the role of notation. I discovered early composers did not include expressive markings. My interpretive ideas had to come from score notation. My emotional connections, activated by the question "why did he or she do that?" permeated my consciousness as I studied the composer's use of harmony, melody, rhythm, and texture. These elements expressed the composer's emotional connection to the text, but how do I project these connections?

The object of this book—achieving inspired rehearsing and performing—is realized through a conductor's understanding of, and connection to the emotional vocabulary of the composer, and the process is completed by the conductor's musicianship and musicality that offers this realization to the choir. I have long believed that notation can block us in our effort to uncover the emotional content necessary to project a communicative response to music. In performance, just reproducing harmonies, rhythms, melodies, and textures may not necessarily mean the choir is singing music.

Acquiring an inspired revelation is a complex process. Realizing symbolic notation in sound requires the conductor's *mind's ear,* the conceptualization of information that the symbols reveal, and all they imply. Bringing this composite picture to aural life requires imagination. Score study is the catalyst that fires the informed imagination. Score study spawns the mental-aural image and is the powerful energizer in rehearsal to motivate singers towards achieving a conductor's concept of the composer's intentions.

It is important to keep in mind that the composer starts with a blank page; we can assume the kernel of inspiration for the composer is the text. Our job is to analyze how the composer illuminates the text, from the total design to details that order its architecture, harmony, melody, rhythm, and texture. This book reinforces how to discover the composer's expressive vocabulary: tempo and tempo change, dynamics, phrasing, articulation, rubato, and linear direction.

Conductors must bring these insights to rehearsal. The goal of the rehearsal is to develop *ensemble,* the unified sound continuum that projects the mental-aural image of the composer's intentions. Achieving ensemble is challenging. It is made possible through unifying pitch, duration, timbre, and intensity: get it in tune, get it in balance, match the vowels, get it together. This achievement creates a unified sound continuum, a clear conduit through which the composer's arsenal of expression can be heard. Once *ensemble* is achieved, choirs can communicatively reveal the emotional meaning of the music.

The core of the choral art is rehearsing. Conductors teach choirs to understand how the structural, stylistic, and expressive elements relate to text meaning. Singers learn how the composition reflects the meaning of the text both broadly and in detail. They realize how a composer illuminates the meaning of a word, creates the mood of a verse or expresses the emotion of a line of text.

Mood, what could be more human than *mood*, especially a sensitivity to changes of mood? Mood sensitivity may be the most important window through which conductors gain insight. We sing to reveal mood, a deeply rewarding experience for singers, conductors, and audiences. In preparing for a performance, the choir imagines how their sound will inspire listeners. The capacity to bring notational symbols to meaningful life boils down to comprehending the composer's emotional communication, the humanity of music.

It is the emotion we feel about a piece of music that motivates us to perform. The emotion is our ultimate energizer, the connection that motivates conductors to develop concepts of a composition to share with a choir, is the goal. Conductors' insights are the catalyst which draws singers closer to experiencing meaningful music making. The resulting inspiration is the catalyst by which we experience the transcendent power of music.

The Personal—Internal Side

Emotion

|

Content

/\

Energy   *Passion*

APPENDICES

—APPENDIX A—

EXPRESSIVITY: EMOTIONS, WORDS, INTERVALS

INTRODUCTION

Making *meaning* out of music is music *making*. We begin with the basics: intervals and their inherent power of emotion. Horizontal and vertical intervals *create* moods.[94] Intervallic relationships inherently convey feelings—*affects* of emotional undercurrents – that first were experienced in singing chant (before notation developed), that eventually evolved into multi-voice medieval music that developed into polyphony by the fourteenth century. The earliest notational symbols preserved in chant were neither notes nor rhythms; they were nuances that reminded singers of the *emotional* expression of chant-singing, the rich treasure trove of melodies that adorned the sacred texts.

Choral repertoire from about the thirteenth century through the late seventeenth century contained no expressive marks; composers (who were directors) knew "how the songs went." Expressive

---

94 See Chapter 15 about moods created by vertical and horizontal intervals and chord progressions.

markings did not appear until the late seventeenth century. Decisions regarding placement of dynamics, phrasing, articulation, linear direction, and rubato, were rarely indicated. Choral compositions always present challenges of ensemble rhythm, intonation, balance, and textural clarity, and in early music where no markings are indicated, expressive nuances must be added to the conductor's responsibility.

By the end of the eighteenth century and especially throughout the nineteenth century and today, we see composers' markings that convey feelings about how the composition should go. Many compositions illustrate an enormous range of composers' sound images; however, the strongest indications of "how it goes" relates most substantially to the compositional vocabulary itself—how the composer highlights the meaning of the text by using melody, harmony, rhythm, and texture to serve it. Despite any markings it is the composer's notation itself that most accurately reveals the emotional connection. Pitch and time are explicit; pitch combinations create changing moods; emotions are guided by intricate combinations of melody and harmony, and implicit moods are implied by the notation, the gestural rhetoric. Application of subtle dynamics, nuanced phrase-groups, articulation, rubato-etched motion with linear direction are to be drawn from the arsenal of expression that can portray the composer's emotional language.

This section of the book presents five varied compositions from the sixteenth, seventeenth, eighteenth, nineteenth, and twentieth centuries with analyses for performance. My primary purpose is to explore how a composer expresses the *moods* of the text, especially created by horizontal and vertical intervals [frequently connected to verbs], and to suggest expressive nuances: dynamics, phrasing, articulation, linear direction, tempo modifications, rubato, and specific recommendations related to tuning, tempo, meter, texture, and balance. Through this viewpoint we can understand how to a) make clear, b) enhance, c) project, d) mirror, e) put into relief, and f) highlight the intended emotional nuance.

In Chapter 12, "Painting with Words," we analyzed Palestrina's motet "Sicut cervus desiderat" and explored specific indications of numerous expressive nuances that bring into relief the *affect* of the text as well as suggestions for expressive nuances related to melody, harmony, rhythm, and texture. Analyses for performance are provided below for five additional works from the seventeenth to the twentieth centuries:

H. Schütz	*Selig sind die Toten*
J. S. Bach	*Wenn ich einmal so scheiden* (chorale, *St. Matthew Passion*)
W. A. Mozart	*Ave verum Corpus*
J. Brahms	*Warum ist das Licht gegeben* (part I)
B. Britten	*The Evening Primrose* from *Five Flower Songs*

REFERENCE RECORDINGS

Included in this book are references to recordings of twelve works I have conducted, available online at [giamusic.com/emotion]. These performances seek to illustrate interpretive ideas related to the expressive nuances that I believe are inherent in the following compositions:

Title	Composer and dates	Choir
1. *Caritas Abundat*	Hildegard of Bingen (1098–1179)	RCS
2. *Alma redemptoris Mater*	Johannes Ockeghem (c. 1410–1497)	HRCM
3. *Sicut cervus desiderat*	Giovanni Pierluigi da Palestrina (1525–1594)	HGC
4. *Ave verum Corpus*	Josquin des Prez (c. 1450–1521)	RCS
5. *O beata et gloriosa Trinitas*	Palestrina	HRCM
6. *When David Heard*	Thomas Tomkins (1592–1656)	HGC
7. *La piaga c'ho nel core*	Claudio Monteverdi (1567–1643)	HRCM
8. *Selig sind die Toten*	Heinrich Schütz (1585–1672)	HRCM
9. *Gazapkhuli*	Georgian Folk Song	HGC
10. *Warum ist das Licht gegeben*	Johannes Brahms (1833–1897)	HRCM
11. *Abendlied*	Josef Rheinberger (1839–1901)	HRCM
12. *Wo ist ein so herrlich Volk*	Brahms	HRCM

Op. 109, No. 3 from *Fest und Gedenkspriche*

Harvard performing ensembles

RCS = Radcliffe Choral Society

HCG = Harvard Glee Club

HRCM = Harvard-Radcliffe Collegium Musicum

We were not able to include recordings of choral-orchestral repertoire, nor works of the twentieth or twenty-first centuries for reasons of copyright and permissions rights.

Heinrich Schütz

Selig sind die Toten
from *Geistliche Chor-Music*

Introduction

Heinrich Schütz (1585–1672) published *Geistliche Chor-Music* in 1648, the year in which the Peace of Westphalia concluded the Thirty Years War. The war had devastated central Europe for three decades, especially the court and church musical establishments. Schütz spent much of his life employed in Dresden as well as traveling throughout Europe. In 1628, he gained permission from Elector Georg of Dresden to travel to study with Monteverdi at St. Mark's in Venice. By 1630 Schütz came back to Dresden to resume compositional duties for court ceremonies. He traveled extensively throughout his lifetime, returning to Dresden for varied responsibility with the court and church musicians. By 1650 Dresden employed nineteen musicians including about three singers per part.

Geistliche Chor-Music contains twelve motets for five-part choir, twelve motets for six-part choir, and five motets for seven vocal parts. Most interestingly, the motets contain no *basso continuo* parts. During the seventeenth century pitch standards varied considerably, primarily related to the inclusion of instruments for court ceremonies or concerted works, and exclusion if performed only in church with organ. Generally, organ pitch (*Chorton*) was high to chamber pitch (*Kammerton*). Modern collected works editions write *Geistliche Chor-Music* almost entirely on G; the original pitch was on F.

Because he writes "it suggests paradoxically an *unaccompanied* performance,"[95] in his Preface to this collection Schütz does suggest that organists can transcribe the motets for the organ. We do not know the pitch of the Dresden organ in the mid- to late-seventeenth century; some scholars believe that it may have been close to *Chorton*. It is well known, however, that during this time church-pitch for choirs varied considerably and choirs would have performed these motets on many pitch standards. That the motets were written primarily on F and that modern editions have transcribe them on G has often suggested to me the decision to perform many motets on F♯, a key that stays far better in tune than F or G.

Below is a quote from Schütz's Preface to *Geistliche Chor-Music* that relates to his reaction to contemporary Italian musical composition, his thoughts about support for no (or little) *basso continuo*, and specifically his thoughts about the loss of composers writing counterpoint—his *raison d'être* for composing and publishing these twenty-nine motets:

> Even the best-trained musician can never properly compose in this new style[96], let alone master it, if he does not thoroughly understand contrapuntal composition. . . Compositions without contrapuntal techniques, even if they sound heavenly to non-musicians, are beneath the skills of experienced composers. Poor compositions are no more valuable than a

---

95 *Heinrich Schütz. Geistliche Chor-Music*, Opus 11 (SWV 369–397), edited by Andrew Thomas Kuster, self-published, Ann Arbor, MI, 2005. This is an extensive and extremely valuable book that Andrew Kuster has written containing transcriptions of all the motets, on F, in the original notation and mensurations (mostly C and 3/1), with invaluable, extensive notes, several tables, Schütz's Preface to the publication, as well as an insightful historical background of Schütz, and translations of all texts.

96 Schütz is referring to German composers that now write in the "modern" Italian style of composition with *basso continuo*; this entire quote is published in German with English translation in Andrew Kuster's edition and preface, cited above.

deaf nut. For this purpose, I was compelled to create a work demonstrating good compositions without basso continuo. Perhaps this will energize emerging German composers in particularly so that, before they compose in the concerted style, they crack this hard nut. This nut contains a kernel of truth: the genuine foundation of good counterpoint.

The reader will have noticed earlier my passionate remarks about performing polyphony and composing polyphony today for conductors, students, and their choirs, offering them the best possible musical education via the development of independence, style, self-confidence, and musicianship.

ANALYSIS FOR PERFORMANCE

The words are from Revelation 14:13 found in the Lutheran Bible.

Selig sind die Toten	Blessed are the dead
die in dem Herren sterben	who die in the Lord.
Nun, ja der Geist spricht	Now, yea the Spirit speaks;
sie ruhen von ihrer Arbeit	they rest from their labors;
und ihrer Werke folgen ihnen nacht	their works do follow them.

In translating Schütz's mind's ear to the choir there are innumerable expressive nuances that can be considered. The basic question is, given insights into Schütz's score, what do we ask of the choir? From the written notation we see many opportunities to improve clarity of tuning, balance, and texture, and there is a range of expressive components that we can use to make aural clarity of Schütz's emotional intentions: dynamics (dynamic/motion), phrasing, articulation, linear direction (dynamic/motion), and rubato (dynamic/motion).

WORDS AND MUSIC—TUNING, BALANCE, LINEAR DIRECTION, DYNAMICS, MOTION

The first twelve measures present varied musical implications for the words *Selig sind die Toten* (Blessed are the Dead). Measures 1–7 create a unity of spirit with a rich sonorous homophonic texture; these majestic measures represent the universality of the adjective and noun *blessed(ness)*. To achieve this unity of spirit, the six vocal parts must be in tune and well balanced to put into relief the inherent beauty and "oneness" of this gesture that can be projected meaningfully by singing a modest crescendo from the opening *Selig* to the "noun-object" *Toten;* tune well the final G major chord.[97]

For the next phrase, *die in dem Herren sterben* (who die in the Lord,) Schütz provides an immediate contrast of texture; the brief overlapping imitative polyphonic lines project the *independence of each person,* and humanity's outcome: to *die* (verb, *sterben*) leading to the object, *Herren.* Singing the quarter notes of each of the ascending lines with a modest *crescendo* with forward motion that leads to *Herren* will highlight meaningfully the *individuality* and the *inevitability* of humanity. A sharp ♯ appears in the alto on *sterben;* in German "sharp" also means "cross."[98] The final chord of this phrase is pitched on B major, a harmony symbolically distant from the opening G major *(Selig).* Tune and balance carefully the two major chords. Let the descending completion of the phrase on m. 12 relax with a modest *diminuendo,* confirming the inherent nuance of an "Amen" plagal (IV–I) cadence.

---

97 Chapters 9 and 13 describe what being in tune means.

98 The sharp sign ♯ relates two words in German: "sharp" and "cross." The cross symbolizes the crucifixion, and is commonly used by German composers of the seventeenth and eighteenth centuries, most noteworthy in Bach's Passions, and many cantatas.

Beginning m. 13, Schütz offers a setting of joy for *selig sind*. Each part overlaps and imitates each other in dance-like triple groups of three quarter notes; the bass projects the "triple" motion in augmentation as all parts approach a brief cadence on *Toten* on E, symbolically containing two sharps. Schütz's imitative dance gestures confirm another emotion inherent in the word, *selig*—"happy." A degree of forward motion will reveal Schütz's "enthusiastic" setting of this brief sequence.

In mm. 19–36, the imitative polyphonic ascending patterns first heard for the text "who die in the Lord" are elongated; this setting meaningfully enhances the emotion of *selig*: "happiness, blessedness, and longing." The length of the phrase seems to magnify humankind's hopeful anticipation of inevitable death. These eighteen measures seem to confirm a reaffirmation of faith, within which brief cadences occur contemplatively.

At m. 37 there is a strikingly strong M7th dissonance that alerts us to a new text: *Nun, ja der Geist spricht* (Now, yea the Spirit speaks); it is a phrygian cadence that expresses a note of sorrow (*Toten*; "the dead") and resolution (*selig*). A single (tenor) voice announces, "Yea, the Spirit speaks"—a strong gesture that projects individuality. We can complement the emotional content of this phrase that Schütz intends by 1) carefully tuning and balancing the M7th dissonance; 2) allowing a subtle ritard and diminuendo at the cadence; and 3) employing individualistic dynamics when the solo tenor line interrupts the phrase.

Schütz's setting of "Yea, the Spirit speaks" (mm. 40–45) has a joyful dramatic meaning; he repeats *der Geist* four times with quick overlapping voices, as if to say, "Listen, listen, listen—the Lord, Lord, Lord, Lord *speaks!*" The long notes are a cry for strength and the repetitive gestures reinforce the feeling of urgency. Tune and balance the series of chords on the verb *spricht*, with pure unisons, octaves, and fifths, and especially the M3rds, that are considerably low to piano equal temperament.

The brief, powerful setting of "the Spirit speaks" (mm. 45–49) is given a poignant resolution by Schütz's beautiful contemplative setting of *sie ruhen* (they rest). "Rest" is portrayed with long slow notes as if time is suspended; these occur on a series of plagal (IV–I) cadences enhancing moods of "tranquility" and "resolution." The *affect* of these moods can be made clear with a calm *diminuendo* and with subtle tempo relaxation from *ru-* to *-hen* each time this gesture occurs.

Immediately following is Schütz's expressive setting of *von ihrer Arbeit* (from their labor). It could not be more vivid! We hear a long series of dissonant passing half-note chords; mm. 49–55 contain vertical note-clusters: D, E, F♯, G, and A, that are initiated by the bass and overlapped by the tenor I, tenor II, alto, and soprano voices. When contrasted with the tranquility of "calmness" of the slow restful IV–I cadences, humanity's "labors" will be made especially dramatic by tuning and balancing the dissonances, clarifying these note clusters. Technically, to receive expressive clarity, the whole steps (D E F♯; and G A) must be tuned very slightly wide to tempered tuning, each chord balanced as they pass in time. The half-steps F♯–G with the crossing two tenor parts, mm. 50–51, will be made *clear* through balancing them, and singing a wide enough interval to confirm the half-step crossings are not out-of-tune unisons.

Between mm. 55–64, Schütz returns to the tranquility of "rest," followed by the "anxiety" of "your labors." This time, Schütz highlights the pronoun (*ihrer*—"your") with many compositional techniques: a) chromaticism—two diminished 4ths: G♯–C and C♯–F (mm. 61 and 63); b) high-ranged dissonances between the two soprano parts; c) a striking series of three suspensions; and d) simultaneously heard in m. 63, the vivid diminished 4th (soprano I, tenor I) with the half-step dissonance (soprano I and alto) that "resolves" immediately to a half-step dissonance between the alto and tenor I. In this manner, Schütz increases the emotional intensity of *ihrer*, ("your" [labor]), giving this pronoun "ownership." Throughout the beautiful consonances of "rest" and the many forms of dissonance (major 7ths, minor 2nds, diminished 4ths) and vocal suspensions, conductors must pay close attention to balance and tuning the individual vocal parts to allow these intervals to reflect the expressive sensitivity intended by Schütz.

Beginning in m. 65, Schütz sets the final phrase of the text *und ihre Werke folgen ihnen nach* ("and their works do follow them") by employing a very different *affect*. Schütz's festive imitative quick-note textures in close canonic imitation highlights the verb "to follow" in an eight-measure "eagerly hurried" style. This wonderful celebration of "for those who die—their works will be remembered" concludes momentarily by the (IV–I) "rest motif" in two imitative 3-part textures (TTB, SSA) that contrastingly amplify this sentiment. The "rewards" of life's struggles are made even more vivid through Schütz's imagination by repeating *sie ruhen von ihrer Arbeit* in the highest range of the entire motet with a full six-part texture (82–84). The rich sonority of the expansive six vocal parts highlights the meaning Schütz seems to intend for all generations whose works will be remembered (85–91), made especially poignant by the long lyric vocal lines peppered with chromaticism and dissonance.

From mm. 65–90, Schütz emphasizes the emotional expressions of "resting," "laboring," and "remembering" by contrasting these moods with the exact same powerful images: a) slow notes on IV–I cadences for "rest;" b) excruciating dissonances for "your labors;" and c) joyful imitative, rhythmic, and quasi dance-like motives for "shall be remembered." Schütz's final seven measures seem to indicate a "summary of faith" and conclude with the two high sopranos imitatively echoing "your works will follow you." The final G major chord contains D as the highest note. Schütz's choice (the 5th of the chord as the highest note) reflects the emotional quality of sound he intends, "forever."

Selig sind die Toten

Performing Edition:
Stuart McIntosh

Heinrich Schütz

4

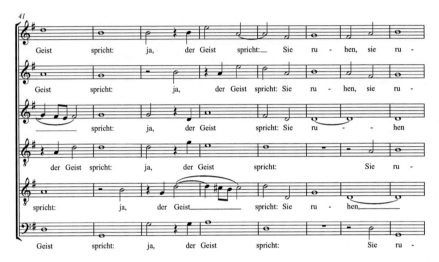

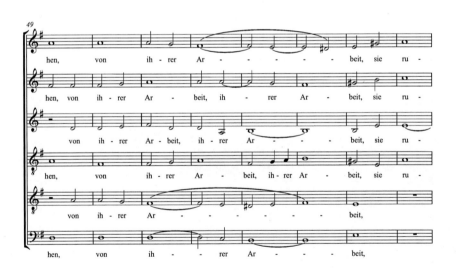

5

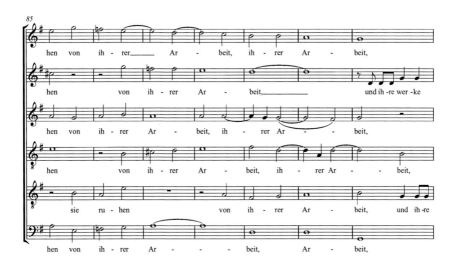

JOHANN SEBASTIAN BACH

WENN ICH EINMAL SOLL SCHEIDEN
(WHEN I ONE DAY MUST DEPART)
MATTHÄUS-PASSION BWV 244, CHORALE #62

The text of Johann Sebastian Bach's (1685–1750) chorale *Wenn ich einmal soll scheiden* is taken from the German translation by the Lutheran hymnist Paul Gerhardt (1607–1675). The original Latin text is from a thirteenth century Passion poem with multiple stanzas addressing the various parts of the body of Christ hanging on the cross. Gerhardt translated ten stanzas of this medieval poem, known best by his translation of the first verse, *O Haupt voll Blut und Wunden,* (O Sacred Head, Now Wounded). The melody was composed by Hans Leo Hassler and is based on his secular song, "Mein G'müt ist mir verwirret" that appeared in a print 1601. Gerhardt's translations, especially of *Wenn ich einmal soll scheiden,* presents a personal contemplation of the events of Christ's death on the cross.

In his *St. Matthew Passion*, Bach wrote five settings of stanzas of the "Passion Hymn." The harmonies Bach employed in his setting of the same melody are harmonically vivid. In this final chorale setting he does not shy away from using dissonance and chromaticism to highlight the emotions of the words. Especially interesting is to observe the key signature of each of the five chorale settings; that tonally descend from four sharps to three flats, to two sharps, to one flat, to none (numbers 15, 17, 44, 54, and 62). As Professor Christoph Wolff points out in his magnificent book, *Johann Sebastian Bach, the Learned Musician*[99], the harmonic construction Bach employs

---

[99] Chapter 9, from the section titled "The 'Great Passion' and Its Context," page 301. Especially riveting is Professor Wolff's entire paragraph from which this small fragment above is taken, in which he describes Bach's exploration of the limits of tonality in several preceding movements, "F-flat minor requiring double flats...B♭-minor, five flats near the bottom end of the circle of fifths, "to the absolute depth of despair," a subsequent transition to E♭-minor (six flats). In "Ach Golgatha," Bach "fully exploits all twelve chromatic pitches."

in the immediate context of this chorale are "at once compellingly expressive and symbolic. . . They are all the more remarkable given the maximum range for a mixed group of instruments not regulated by equal temperament."

During the course of Bach's *St. Matthew Passion* he employs twenty-three of the twenty-four major and minor keys. His key choices rest upon the ongoing picture of the passion scenes he portrays, especially to highlight the emotions of the words of the passion story through vivid reflections. Portraying his disciples, Bach set twelve chorales, each humanly empathetic to the ongoing drama. Bach's choices of keys and harmonies are aligned with the slow changing emotional topics: Jesus' love; man's guilt; Christ's sweetness; man's loyalty, faith, and empathy; Christ's mercy and grace; man's faith and innocence; Christ's betrayal, mocking, forgiveness of sins; and acceptance of the cross.

BACH'S INHERENT EXPRESSIVE SYMBOLS
SYMBOLS AND WORD-MUSIC RELATIONSHIPS

mm. 1–4   Wenn ich einmal soll scheiden,
               So scheide nicht von mir;
                    When I one day must depart,
                    then do not depart from me;
               Wenn ich den Tod soll leiden,
               So tritt du denn herfür;
                    When I death shall suffer,
                    step you then to me;

mm. 5–8   Wenn mir am allerbängsten
               Wird um das Herze sein,
                    When to me a great fear
                    will constrict about my heart

mm. 9–12   So reiß mich aus den Ängsten
                  Kraft deiner Angst und Pein!
                  Then snatch me from my anxieties,
                  by the power of your fear and suffering!

MEASURES 1–4

- The lowest key of the five Passion chorales
- The descending line of the bass leading to the lowest note (F♯) occurring on a diminished 5th from C);
- The ♯ sign symbolizes departing (*scheiden*) *and* suffering (*leiden*) on the cross; "sharp" means "cross" in German
- "*So*" turn of the phrase on G♯ (diminished 4th, and "cross") galvanizing our pleas, "do not leave me, stand beside me"
- *Scheide nicht* and *tritt du* (verbs: depart not; stand you) made glowingly apparent by Bach's personal ornament of the chorale melody on "de" of *Schei-de* by adding an eighth note and two sixteenths—quick notes on the word "depart."

MEASURES 5–8

- *mir* (me—Christ) the "double cross": F♯ and D♯ (preceded by diminished 5th)
- *allerbängsten* (full of fear/anxiety): six accidentals; home key of A minor becomes momentarily unanchored with consecutive dominants of e minor, B♭ major, C, and subdominant with a flat 3rd of C. The momentary hint of B♭ major creates a *clear* disorientation from both A minor and C major; and with chromaticism in alto, tenor, bass.
- *wird um das Herze sein* (shall constrict my heart): more "anxiety" created by hint at returning to F (through C7) followed by "constrict," the major 7th dissonance on *um*

sliding to momentary C♯ diminished and G minor 6/4, to *Herze sein* hinting at A major preceded by the alto E forming a "cruel" minor 2nd dissonance against the soprano.

MEASURES 9–12

- *so reiß mich* (so snatch me); A major is not confirmed; harmonies drawn to *mich* (tenor ornamented=ownership) to G followed by three chords "wresting me" from *"den Ängsten"* (the terrors).
- *Kraft deiner Angst und Pein* ([by the] strength of your anguish and pain.) Strength: C major, G7, C major (security of) your anguish and pain: five accidentals that return purposefully to the E major chord, the dominant of A minor, therefore remaining unresolved until Christ dies on the cross.

BACH'S MUSIC AND WORDS: EXPRESSION

Bach's twelve-measure chorale, *Wenn ich einmal soll scheiden,* is laden with emotional moments of *change*: in key, harmony, melody, rhythm, and texture, made dramatically intense with the dissonance, chromaticism, linear ornaments, suspensions, and appoggiaturas. How might we apply these characteristics of expression to clarify Bach's conception? We can achieve this a) by tuning and balancing the SATB vocal parts, and b) by using dynamics, phrasing, articulation, linear direction, and rubato related to Bach's heightening of the text through his emotional expression of it.

BALANCE AND TUNING

Bach creates very specific intervals in order to highlight the mood of the passing text. A frequently neglected ingredient, and an essential one, is to clarify specific vertical intervals by achieving excellence of balance and tuning.

Bach sets this final Passion chorale in the lowest key of the five preceding chorales, and therefore balance considerations occur throughout the twelve measures. The bass low notes must balance (especially the tenor) in m. 2 the F♯, G♯; and in mm. 10–11 the low G, G♯; these four examples, will require strong vocal support from the other voices to balance the tenor part, written a 10th above the bass. With the exception of the tenor part, the low ranges of the sopranos and altos require attention to balance the tenor especially mm. 2, 8, 9–10 of the sopranos, and mm. 1, 2, 11–12 of the altos. The alto parts can be balanced by adding high tenors in m. 1, 2, 11, and 12 by high baritones. If several tenors sing the alto in measures 1, 2, and 11, it may be important to add one or two baritones to the tenor part in m. 12. Adding a few altos to the soprano in those measures might be helpful.

Balance and intonation are extremely important in clarifying minor 2nds and major 7ths ; compared to tempered tuning of the piano, major 7ths must be sung slightly narrow and minor 2nds slightly wide.[100] For example, in m. 7 on the word *um,* the E of the alto and F of the bass must be sung narrow to disavow this interval from being an out-of-tune octave. The *"-ze"* in *Herze* must be slightly wide to clarify that F and E together is not an out-of-tune unison.

FERMATAS

We now know that in Leipzig in the Thomaskirche, Bach's Passion settings in performance did not include congregational singing; however, what other guidelines might we follow today? The eight

---

100 See Chapter 10

chorales of *St. Matthew Passion* display an enormous range of uncommon harmonizations that reveal Bach's expressive sensitivity towards the words, and most likely how he felt his composition should represent the mood of the words and specific emotions of the passing text. Like all chorale settings in his sacred works there are no expression marks, except fermatas (caesuras). In this context a looming question arises: how do we interpret the fermatas in *Wenn ich einmal*?

Five of the eight chorales that Bach set in the *St. Matthew Passion* are called Passion Chorales. These are based on a long medieval Latin poem mourning Christ on the Cross. Paul Gerhardt's 1556 German version was widely adopted in sacred Baroque works. Bach set five verses based on Gerhardt's translation. *Wenn ich einmal soll scheiden* is the most dramatic of the five. Like each of his chorales the nature of the setting is entirely related to the poetic drama of the words, especially in the context of the Passion story. Bach's Passion settings reflect in essence an ongoing music-drama, filled with calculated, extremely diverse moods; the form, harmony, melody, rhythm, and texture structure support it. In this light, we may consider many kinds of *caesuras*: a full pause, a brief break, a breath coinciding with the comma, or a slight resignation of silence. These nuances will inevitably relate to the approach to the fermatas and the continuation of the phrase after the fermata. The approach and continuation both relate to expression, employing to one degree or another dynamics, phrasing, articulation, and rubato.

Fermata interpretations relate to the phrase-moods that precede and follow them. Appropriate expressive nuances to highlight Bach's poignant setting of words within the phrases, framed by the fermatas, include natural syllabic stress, dynamic inflection, vocal articulation of ornamented notes, and carrying the phrase with linear direction and relaxation (*tempo rubato*).

Verse one:

Measures 1–4: *When I one day must depart, then do not depart from me.* The fermata exists in the middle of two phrases; a brief breath seems appropriate.

Measures 1 and 2: begins in a low range; soprano, bass in a parallel descending direction; alto, tenor ascending 8th notes lead to m. 2, the object: *depart* with alto appoggiatura, and F♯ bass (augmented 4th.) A syllabic stress on *schei-* complements this gesture; the dynamic level of mm. 1 and 2 calls for an expressive *mp*.

Measures 3 and 4: begins with a diminished 4th, C–G♯ bass, with a higher soprano range and ornament on *scheide;* vocal articulation will clarify this possessive verb. The phrase gesture suggested will be complimented by a modest *crescendo* and forward motion to *nicht*—a pointed interrogative, concluding with the soprano and alto paired appoggiatura on *von* that will require word-stress mirroring the sense of "ownership": don't depart *von mir.*

Verse two:

Musical repetition of verse one; text becomes more dramatic.

Measures 1–4: The part of the rhymed phrase musically repeats the first; the emotions heat up: "when I must suffer death," sing *mp+ to mf-;* "come you to me!" sing *schei- mf-* moving to *nicht, mf,* followed by a slight *diminuendo* to *mir.*

Verse three:

Measures 5–8: "When I most full of fear that constricts my heart." The fermata is placed in the middle of two modifying clauses; this suggests to connect the modifiers: no breath or a quick catch-breath.

Measures 5–8: Syllabic stresses on strong beats—*mir, al, bäng; um, Her, sein*—reflect Bach's purposeful emphasis. The diminished 5th, bass A to D♯, is followed by 2 chromatic measures that create harmonic instability that amps up the phrase tension. Crescendo *mp* to *mf* with forward motion on *al-ler-bäng* to highlight Bach's gesture, followed by a slight *ritard* on the tenor A♭ preceding *sten*.

Measures 11–12 begin to resolve the tension, though the chromaticism, major 7th F/E (bass and alto) and minor 2nd dissonance (soprano and alto), that highlight *um* and *Herze* (constricted heart) are both worth an imploring dynamic gesture of stress/release leading to the appoggiatura on *sein*. Dynamics throughout mm. 7–8 should be a steady *mf*.

Verse four:

Measures 9–12: "Then snatch me from my anxieties by the power of your fear and suffering." The fermata on *Ängsten* occurs at the height of the drama; the final two measures seem to dissolve into a quality of contemplative hope. This textual apposition requires a relatively full pause on the fermata. Bach confirms this idea by placing the fermata on a widely spaced chordal texture that is followed by vocal leaps of a 5th to the next chord in closed position. A breath before *Kraft* leads naturally to the final phrase, an unwinding of Bach's dramatic setting of the chorale text.

Measures 9–10: Bach portrays *me* (object of *snatch*) with the tenor ornamenting *mich*, providing a signal of "ownership;" sing *mich* with clear articulation. Measures 9–10 are filled with passing 8th note motion leading to *Ängsten*. (Note the bass diminished 5th to C♯ on *Ängsten*, which is the center of a phrase containing three "sharps," that mean "cross" in German.) *Snatch me from anxieties* requires the strongest dynamics (*mf–* to *f–*) with considerable forward motion that will heighten the drama, reaffirmed by the alto suspension on *Äng-*. Allow the full emotional impact of this phrase by holding the fermata on *sten*.

Measures 11–12: *by the power of your fear and suffering*—the SATB wide vocal texture on the fermata that moves to the closed-position chord on *Kraft,* speaks most meaningfully by juxtaposing a change in dynamics c. *f* to c. *mp+*. The emotions of "fear and suffering" of the final two measures are reflected in Bach's harmonically vague chromaticism that leads to a concluding *affect* on the chord of the final fermata. It is a half cadence: a questioning representation of Christians maintaining the *hope* of the *affect* of the entire chorale for Christ's comforting presence to us when we die, taking away our fear by remembering his poignant example. A mood of prayerful *hope* can be beautifully achieved by a continuous *diminuendo* to the final fermata *p, pp, ppp, niente*. The two sharps on *Pein* may be Bach's symbol of Judas's "double-cross."

Due to his thorough and scrupulous revisions, "the definitive character of Bach's 1736 revision of the *St. Matthew Passion* [offer us] no comparable manuscript score from Bach's hand."[101] Also according to Wolff, "It could not be more evident that in 1736 Bach considered this score as his most significant work."[102]

101 Christoph Wolff, *Ibid*, p.298
102 Ibid, p. 298

Matthäus-Passion BWV 244

62. Choral: Wenn ich einmal soll scheiden

Johann Sebastian Bach (1685–1750)

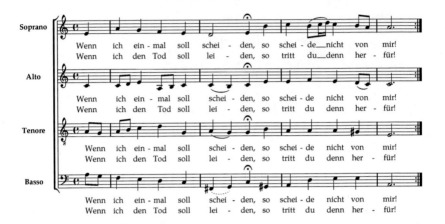

WOLFGANG AMADEUS MOZART
AVE VERUM CORPUS, K. 618

HISTORICAL NOTES

Wolfgang Amadeus Mozart (1756–1791) composed *Ave verum Corpus* in 1791 for Anton Stoll, church choirmaster in Baden-Baden (a small town near Vienna), while visiting his wife Constanze, who was enjoying Baden's spa. *Ave verum Corpus* honors the Feast of Corpus Christe, June 23 (1791), that commemorates Christ's sacrament of redemption. The words and setting focus on the Christian rite of Eucharist, the flow of water and blood from Jesus' pierced side. The manuscript source of *Ave verum Corpus* confirms Baden June 17, 1791.

> *Ave verum Corpus natum de Maria Virgine:*
>> Hail, true body, born of Mary Virgin:
>
> *Vere passum immolatum in cruce pro homine.*
>> truly suffered, sacrificed on cross for mankind.
>
> *Cujus latus perforatum, unda fluxit et sanguine:*
>> Whose side was pierced, water flowed and blood:
>
> *Esto nobis praegustatum in mortis examine.*
>> before us a foretaste of (heaven) examining death.

Ave verum Corpus is written in a four-part homophonic style that offers a compact and transparent clarity. This motet is Mozart's first choral composition without reference to *stile antico,* the old polyphonic style that was required for composers of church compositions in the eighteenth century, both his predecessors and contemporaries. Composed less than six months before his death, it foreshadows many stylistic aspects of his *Requiem,* especially its declamatory gestures and homophonic textures. In essence it is a new style in contradistinction to the traditional *stile antico.*

STYLISTIC FEATURES

The *Adagio* mark and *alla breve* ₵ sign signal Mozart's ideas for tempo, phrasing, and mood. *Adagio* means "at ease, leisurely"; ₵ in Mozart's era marks the natural phrase points—the down beats. The tempo of *Adagio* in Classic music is c. 54–60, related to the quarter note in this composition due to the *alla breve* sign. The string parts with organ continuo double the harmonies of the choir with the exception of one brief interlude and the two 2-measure phrases opening and closing the work.

The natural Latin word stresses coincide with two pulses per measure; they seem to suggest a gentle rocking motion. *Sotto voce* appears eight times in the score. *Sotto* means "under or below," having a clear connotation of "somewhat soft, serene, perhaps subdued," yet by no means without expression. While dynamic marks do not appear in the original parts, Mozart's expressive harmonies and changes of texture invite dynamic accommodations.

Mozart presents each of the four poetic lines of *Ave verum Corpus* in a simple, direct manner coupled with an expressive harmonic vocabulary. Concluding each of the four lines there appear these syllabically rhymed couplets: Vir-*gi-ne*/ho-*mi-ne;* san-*gui-ne*/ex-a-*mi-ne.* Mozart's setting within each line provides increasing harmonic tension that draws us to the final words of each line. This "draw" suggests direction—a sense of forward motion applied sensitively within the text-phrases and measure groupings over the twelve measures of each line, accompanied with increasing dynamic undulation to project Mozart's sorrowful and dramatic setting.

TEXT PHRASES AND MEASURE GROUPINGS

Rhyme scheme—final words of couplets: *Virgine, homine, sanguine, examine*
Text phrases, syllabic stresses, bar groups, half-note pulses. Vertical line shows 2-bar phrase

meas.
1–2 (instruments only)

3–6   A- ve, a- ve | ve- rum   Cor-   pus | Hail, true Body
       2 2 2 2   2 2   2   2   *4 bars, symmetric phrases*

7–10   na-   tum   de Ma-   ri- a | Vir-   gi- ne. | born of Virgin Mary
       2 2   2   2   2 2   2 2   *4 bars, symmetric phrases*

11–14 Ve-   re pas-   sum | im- mo-   la- tum   in | truly suffered, sacrificed
       2 2   2   2   2 2   2 2   *4 bars, symmetric phrases*

15–18 cru-   (in cru-)   ce pro | ho-   mi- ne | (strings) on cross for mankind
       2   2 2   2   2 2   2 2   *4 bars + 3 bars = asymmetric phrase*

       16 bars conclude 1st rhymed verse; 3-bar instruments only = asymmetry

22–25 Cu-   jus la- tus | per-   fo- ra- tum | (strings) on cross for mankind
       2 2   2 2   2 2   2 2   *4 bars, symmetric phrases*

26–29 un-   da flu-   xit et | san-   gui-   ne | flowed water and blood
       2 2   2   2   2 2   2 2   *4 bars, symmetric phrases*

30–33 es -   to no- bis | prae- gu-   sta-   tum   in | be for us a foretaste
       2 2   2 2   2 2   2   2   *4 bars, symmetric phrases*

34–37 mor-   (sta-tum in)   mor-   tis ex- | a-   mi- ne in   (3 bars strings) of death's examining
       2   2   2   2   2 2   2 2   *4 bars, symmetric phrases*

       16 bars conclude 2nd rhymed verse

38–42 mor- | -   tis ex- | a-   mi-   ne
       2 2 2 2   2 2 2   2   2 2   2 2

                                              (3 bars strings) of death's examining
                                              6 bar extension; symmetric phrase
                                              3 bars of strings = asymmetric final phrase

The phrase groups and syllabic stresses of each line above clarify three symmetric twelve-measure groups plus one asymmetric group at the end of line four, *in mortis examine,* where he repeats this emotional text, and concludes the motet with the strings and organ continuo. The repetition plus the orchestral conclusion provides a nine-measure asymmetric phrase. Asymmetric phrase lengths are not uncommon in Mozart's compositional style, and this one including a six-measure repetition of the profound text seems to create an "incomplete" subtle suggestion of "is this all?"

MOZART'S SYMBOLIC NOTATION: CHANGE IN FORM, HARMONY, MELODY, RHYTHM, TEXTURE

The four lines of Latin text contain strong/weak syllabification; these can be expressively projected by offering subtle dynamic stress on "strong" syllables. In this way, the twelve-pulse symmetry of the first three lines of text will be made clear while projecting ever increasing tension throughout changes in harmony and texture. Mozart increases the length of the final fourth line-phrase by repeating the final three words, thereby emphasizing the poignancy of the text.

Throughout the motet Mozart employs chromaticism and dissonance on many beat combinations. Downbeats often contain appoggiatura dissonances; note especially the same vertical harmonies in measures 6 (*Corpus:* body of Christ) and 9 (*Virgine:* his mother). Simultaneous appoggiaturas and dissonances appear frequently with ♯ signs [in German, ♯ sharp means *cross*]; these appear on the note G in m. 4 *Ave* ("hail" [true body]) and m. 12 *passum* ("suffered"), revealing the same melodic motion by the soprano. Continued G♯s all relate to Christ on the cross: m. 13 *immolatum* ("sacrifice"), m. 15 *in cruce* ("on the cross"), m. 28 *sanguine* ("blood"), m. 35 *examine* (humanity's examining), m. 42 *mortis* ("death").

SYMBOLISM

The third line of the text is harmonically remarkable: *Cujus latus perforatum unda fluxit et sanguine* ("whose side was pierced, flowed water and blood"); Mozart leaves the keys of D and A major and modulates from A to F major, a modal progression, that has the emotional *affect* of neither here nor there—impermanence, perhaps symbolizing by the return to A major that His life is not yet gone.

Mozart also dramatically emphasizes mm. 30–37 (before us, (is) a foretaste of heaven, at death examined, at the final hour) with the tenor/bass canonic duet at the fifth with the prior soprano/alto one measure removed. Not only do these eight measures create seven vertical dissonances, concluding with a (symbolic) deceptive (hasn't yet happened) cadence in m. 37, but there are three other important symbols: 1) a *canon* is a *law;* "before us is a foretaste of heaven in the final hour, prior to death; the law confirms inevitable death; and 2) the *canon* occurs at the interval of a fifth. For centuries of Christianity, especially witnessed in Medieval and Renaissance music, the use of harmonic mathematical proportions is symbolic: God = 1:1 unison (there is one God), Father 2:1 octave (God, the Father), and Son 3:2 fifth (Christ, subject of the motet); 3) during the final three words *in mortis examine,* Mozart emphasizes the poignancy of the text with considerable dissonance and rather extreme chromaticism. In fact, the C♮, B♭, and F♮ of mm. 23–28 return, and Mozart adds a D♯ and G♯ (*the cross*) during the six measure repeat of "examining death" (*mortis examine*). These five chromatic notes, not belonging to D or A major, and in the context of their occurring in an asymmetric phrase preceded by a deceptive cadence to G in m. 37, seems purposeful: confirming Christ's death yet leaving room for Christian faith in His return.

There are other interesting points to be made about the final seventeen measures. In measures 30–37 Mozart is paying homage to old-style polyphony by pairing S and A, mirrored two beats later by the TB duet down a fifth; thus, the duets create a polyphonic texture. The TB duet begins one measure after the SA duet and the tenor and bass sing words that do not coincide vertically with the words of the soprano and alto. The "duet polyphony" creates a double function: a) the imitation is clear yet the repetition of the text reinforces the emotions of the words one beat after they were initially heard; and b) therefore, over thirteen measures the vertical sonority contains dissimilar words. By this method Mozart writes expressive appoggiaturas, dissonances, and chromaticism that highlight the emotional meanings of the vertical sonorities and of the whole text.

In conclusion Mozart creates a nine-measure extension in which the final words repeat: *in mortis examine,* "in death's examining (hour)." That text summarizes the meaning of the whole *Ave verum Corpus* text—the hymn in honor of the Blessed Sacrament. The emotion is emphasized by stretching the last three words over seven measures. This nine-measure extension creates an asymmetric phrase that seems purposefully to leave the mood unresolved.

Expression through Tuning, Balance, Vowels, Dynamics, Phrasing, Articulation, and Rubato[103]

Each of the circumstances discussed above require careful tuning, balance, and matched vowels in vertical sonorities. Minor 2nds must

---

103 In the second half of the eighteenth century there were two types of *rubato:* a) a melodic motion against a steady bass part—Mozart was a master pianist of this type of rubato; b) a modest motion of all parts to reinforce structure. Both types are for expressive purposes, and are especially suitable for vertical structures. It is interesting to note that among Haydn, Mozart, and Beethoven, Mozart was the only one to include in his many letters the term *tempo rubato.* Haydn and Mozart appear to use *rubato* in some of their late works for expressive purposes. By 1800, Beethoven indicated *tempo rubato* in his scores. *Adagio* tempi in word-related vertical structures of all three composers are especially inviting for their inclusion of *tempo rubato* in performance.

be made wide and major 7ths must be made narrow (to tempered tuning[104]) to clarify the exact pitch. Vertical dissonances will be heard best with a subtle dynamic stress resolving to a consonance. Linear chromaticism must be defined by careful attention to unified intonation, complemented by subtle dynamic stress and forward motion.

Mozart's homophonic texture requires careful adjustments to balance SATB vocal parts. The vertical textures frequently range within an octave and a fifth; any two vocal parts that are close together can be well balanced by re-voicing them. In mm. 30–36, the tenor and bass parts easily over-balance the soprano and alto parts they are imitating. To clarify the expressive nuances Mozart intends, careful vertical tuning must be adjusted to make clearly audible the dissonance; observing careful text declamation will be imperative in this context. The first three lines of text each contain the same groupings, ongoing motions of two quarter notes (strong-weak) of three continuous patterns that build tension. The cumulative effect suggests ongoing dynamic continuity. Following each of the three lines, Mozart writes four-measure phrases. Longer units create longer tension; the tension again is best served by subtle dynamic stress and forward motion, mirroring the cumulative tension of the text/music relationships. These modest dynamic and rubato inflections will confirm the inherent direction within the twelve-measure phrases expressively.

Mozart's profoundly beautiful, simple, direct, and expressive setting throughout of *Ave verum Corpus* implies continuous gentle forward motion in each long line-phrase. The words are set in common patterns; the harmonies are not. They are varied throughout serving Mozart's expressive vocabulary of dissonance,

---

104 See Chapters 10 and 11 for specific references to tuning.

chromaticism, and appoggiaturas. The sensitivity to the words that Mozart writes cumulatively phrase by phrase can be made apparent in choral performance through caring for the implied gestures of meaningful phrasing, expressive dynamics, and subtle rubato, phrase by phrase. Tuning and balancing vertical sonorities are a prerequisite for building security for Mozart's vocabulary of expression.

Motette
"AVE VERUM CORPUS"
(Kochel No. 618)

W. A. Mozart
(1750 - 1791)

© 1999 Vladimir Ursic

- 3 -

JOHANNES BRAHMS

WARUM IST DAS LICHT GEGEBEN DEM MÜHSELIGEN
OP. 74, NR. 1 (1879)

STYLISTIC KNOWLEDGE—HISTORICAL BACKGROUND

Johannes Brahms (1833–1897) composed *Warum ist das Licht gegeben* in the summer of 1878 and it was published in 1878 with a second motet, *O Heiland, reiss die Himmel auf* that he had composed earlier (c. 1863–1864). The publication of the opus 74 motets was dedicated to the great scholar Philipp Spitta (1841–1894), the author of the first comprehensive work on J. S. Bach.

Brahms' library reflects his life-long interest in the polyphonic music of the Renaissance and Baroque, especially those of Palestrina, Giovanni Gabrieli, Schütz, and the choral works of Handel and Bach. Brahms met Robert and Clara Schumann in 1853 and shared with them his numerous copies of Renaissance motets, German folk songs and chorales, as well as his collection of many performance manuals of the 17th and 18th centuries. On Christmas, 1855, Clara gave Brahms the first volume of Bach *Werke*.

By 1866 he was studying counterpoint, especially of Bach's cantatas; and canons in the lieder of Isaac, Lassus, Praetorius; and motets of Gabrieli, Eccard, and Schütz. By the end of his life Brahms' library contained the complete works of Schütz, as well as most of the works of Gabrieli and his contemporaries. In studying Schütz's motets he especially liked the clever imitation, diminution, text illustrations, striking and unexpected harmonies, expressive chromaticism and dissonance, and use of diminished 4ths and cross relations. "For the rest of his life the arrival of each volume of Bach's complete works was an event of great importance to me," Brahms says, "I particularly love the suspensions in Bach's music, and want them played so as to give the fullest possible effect to the dissonance."[105]

Brahms divides the complete motet *Warum ist das Licht gegeben* into four sections on biblical texts: Job 3:20–23; Lamentations 3:41; James 5:11; and Martin Luther's chorale text. His biblical selections are from the Old and New Testament; they generally represent his philosophical orientation towards death, ranging from: Job's mournful words, the comforting words from Lamentations, to James' writings on *blessedness* by *endurance,* concluding with Martin Luther's words of comfort, *with peace and joy according to God's will.*

Movement 1. Job 3:20–23[106]

Warum ist das Licht gegeben dem Mühseligen,	Why is light given to the miserable, and life to the afflicted soul,
und das Leben den betrübten Herzen,	(before those death waits for and it comes not,
die des Todes warten und kommt nicht,	and dig it well secretly, they nearly rejoice and are glad,
und grüben ihn wohl aus dem Verborgenen,	that they the grave obtain),
die sich fast freuen und sind fröhlich,	and to the man, whose way hidden is and God from him himself has hidden?
daß sie das Grab bekommen,	
und dem Manne, deß Weg verborgen ist,	
und Gott vor ihm denselben bedecket?	

105 Virginia Hancock, *Brahms's Choral Compositions and His Library of Early Music.* (Ann Arbor: UNI Research Press, 1983), 153.

106 Ron Jeffers, trans. and comp., *Translations and Annotations of Choral Repertoire, Volume II: German Texts,* ed. Gordon Paine (Corvallis, OR: earthsongs, 1988).

STRUCTURE, STYLE, TEXT-MUSIC RELATIONSHIPS

An analysis of Brahms' setting of Job 3 (mm. 1–84) will relate to style, structure, and word-music relationships, and how choirs can project Brahms' rich harmonic, melodic, rhythmic, and textural palate with expressive gestures, to amplify Brahms' mind's ear in setting this text.

The first 84 measures of *Warum* Brahms divides into four musical segments. Throughout each we see a poignant representation of the *affect* of the text and the mood of individual words. Each segment is framed with the word *Warum* (Why). Brahms' dynamic marks of each set suggest two emotions: outrage/anger (*f* ≥), resignation/contemplation (*p*). Through his setting of the first two lines of Job he highlights the emotion of two words: *Mühseligen* (those in misery) with ◁ ▷, and *betrübten* (to the afflicted) with 7-note sinuous chromaticism. Brahms sets the first two lines (mm. 1–20) of Job in a strict canon at the 4th; voices enter sequentially from soprano to bass.

The setting of these two lines of text (and nearly all of Job 3) contains the highest degree of chromaticism among Brahms' motets. Beginning with the soprano canonic subject mm. 4–10, Brahms writes within seven measures a twelve-tone row, and the strict SATB canonic contrapuntal texture continues to m. 20. *Canon* in church tradition means *law*, and the philosophy underlying these two lines of text are textually equally relevant throughout verse one, confirming the Lutheran philosophy—humanity endures the pathos of life, and awaits death as the comforting end of life's journey.

Brahms' twelve-tone melody in each SATB part, is a canon that is eight measures long. The soprano begins on d, initiating the twelve tones: *d, d♯, e, f, f♯, g, g♯, a, b♭, b, c, c♯*. At m. 11 the soprano begins a new twelve-tone subject at the repetition of *den betrübten Herzen* beginning on "a." The repetition of the new canon begins with the alto at m. 14 (3rd beat); the tenor at m. 19 (3rd beat), and the bass completes the original canon at m. 20. Overlapping mm. 18–20, the soprano repeats the opening two measures (3–4) up a 5th from the bass (beginning at 14). It is interesting to note the words Brahms chooses to repeat over and over: *den betrüben Herzen* (to the bitter/ afflicted of heart), mm. 11–20, three times in the soprano and alto, twice in the tenor.

The canonic polyphony concludes at m. 20, but *den betrüben Herzen* is drawn out to m. 24 with an alto/tenor duet, followed by soprano/bass, in *canonic* imitation; *law* (in a different form) *is confirmed*; Framing verse 1, Brahms repeats the homorhythmic SATB *Warum* $f \gg p$ and repeats the pitifully sad, *Warum?* with *p*. Through this 24-measure texture, Brahms creates a very high degree of chromaticism and dissonance, aurally symbolic of the questions, "why is light given to those in misery," and "life to those bitterly afflicted of heart."

At the beginning of the first 24 measures of *Warum* Brahms writes the descriptive adjectives: *Langsam und ausdrucksvoll*—"Slowly (broadly) and full of expression." *Langsam und ausdrucksvoll* are ideally suited for highlighting the emotions of the entire section, specifically the tempo, phrasing, and moods that Brahms expects the choir to reflect as they sing the first verse of Job. *Slow* or *broad* also coincide with the natural syllabic stress that occurs on the half-note pulse throughout the entire setting of Job 3:20–22. Singing broadly, expansively with expression are appropriate adjectives to employ throughout mm. 1–84.[107]

---

107 In this context, it is interesting to look back to Brahms' detailed study of the sacred works of Schütz, in particular his 1648 *Geistliche Chormusik*. Brahms received the complete works of Schütz throughout his lifetime and studied the motets in considerable detail. Schütz's motet "Ich Weiss, Erlöser lebt dass mein" from *Geistliche Chormusic* contains the word *Tarde*, one of the very first seventeenth-century appearances of a *word* to describe tempo change. *Tarde* and *langsam* have the same meanings: *slowly* or *broadly*. Schütz's motet contains six proportional tempo changes from **C** to 3/1 (3 whole notes = 1 whole note). Writing *Tarde* at the conclusion of the motet allows Schütz to be free of the proportional **C** to 3/1 relationship, that signals to singers that his motet should slow down as they approach the conclusion. *Tarde* with the **C** sign confirms that the half-note coincides with the syllabic stress of the text. "Broadly" with Brahms' **C** sign also confirms the natural syllabic stress that coincides with the half-note pulse throughout the first 3 verses of Job, up to m. 54.

While *ausdrucksvoll* (full of expression) pertains to his setting of all four verses, Brahms reinforces *full of expression* with two other written emotions: *dolce* (32 and 47) and *espressivo* (m. 43). *Dolce* is first written above *und kommt nicht* ("it comes not"), describing the mood Brahms desires following the words, *Die des Todes wartem* ("those who long for death") in mm. 28–31. *Dolce* is also written with ⤡⤢, a "sigh of disappointment"; the apex of ⤡⤢ occurs at the alto/bass major 7th dissonance E/F, a "sigh of resignation"; Brahms writes *espressivo* at m. 43 that pertains to the four measures: *die sich fast freuen und sind fröhlich* (they nearly rejoice and are glad) leading to the second *dolce* at *daß sie das Grab bekommmen* (that they the grave have *almost* obtained). A two-measure diminuendo concludes the text, emphasizing again "not obtaining the grave." This expressive gesture is immediately followed by the cry of outrage, disappointment, and resignation: "Why? Warum?" sung *f* > and *p*.

Warum ist das Licht gegeben dem Mühseligen	Why is light given to the miserable,
Und das Leben den betrübten Herzen	and life to the afflicted soul,

TUNING, BALANCE, AND CHOOSING EXPRESSIVE PRIORITIES IN MEASURES 1–24

In the first twenty-four measures of *Warum* Brahms creates an extreme high degree of chromaticism and dissonance that directly serves specific words and the emotions of the text, "why is light given to those in misery" and "life to those bitterly afflicted of heart." In this light, these canonic phrases are very difficult to sing! Each twelve-tone canon is comprised of repeated melodic intervals that are difficult to sing in tune: 1) minor 2nds , twelve of them in the first complete twelve-tone melody (imitated by the alto, tenor, bass), and 2) the alternating melodic series of minor and major 2nds (mm. 7–10, soprano, imitated throughout) are especially difficult to sing.

Note the anguish of the text, "and life to the bitter afflicted of heart," that matches the difficulty of the intervals. Throughout the twenty-measure canonic melody, the alto, tenor, and bass repeat the text on the same melodic intervals seven times. Moreover, as a result of these extremely chromatic SATB melodies, the vertical harmonies are especially difficult to tune and to balance. While making decisions about the application of *expressive elements*—dynamics, phrasing, articulation, linear direction, and rubato—the priority first of all is to make this thick texture clear: *tuning and balancing the voice*s is the primary key.

The goal of the conductor is to make these four parts *clear!* How can we accomplish that? Far more than most compositions that choral directors will encounter, *Warum ist das Licht gegeben* (especially the first twenty-four measures) serves up a multitude of challenges to enable Brahms' thick texture to gain clarity, especially because there are internal conflicting goals:

1. *intonation*: horizontal and vertical;
2. *balance*: horizontal and vertical;
3. Brahms' *dynamics*: projecting them in the context of 1 and 2;
4. highlighting inherent (unwritten) *expressive elements* (above) in the context of 1, 2, 3;
5. projecting text declamation of *consonants;* and
6. preserving on going attention to the consistent *syllabic stresses* of the German text.

To accomplished these goals, decisions regarding priorities among the conflicting goals must be made. The specific attention to tuning and balancing over twenty-four measures will require a conductor's careful preparation in advance of rehearsals, to highlight the priorities to project textural clarity. How? Choose one element at a time among each "conflict" that most directly serves the aural meaning of Brahms' text/music relationship; then sort it out and prepare your ear to place the prioritized "conflict" as the primary auditory goal.

The priorities over the first twenty-four measures of *Warum* relate to Brahms' compositional setting of certain text-phrases and specific words within a phrase. Phrase one: *Licht, ge-ge-ben, Müh-se-li-gen* – for each word or syllable—"light, given, (to the) miserable"—Brahms provides the high note of the phrase, plus his expressive $\underset{}{<\quad>}$ on "the miserable." Maintaining the audibility of Brahms' setting in each voice throughout the first twenty measures will be an important priority. The same priority must also be given to phrase two: *Le-ben, be-trüb-ten, Her-zen, den be-trü-ten Her-zen.* In the context of the harmonic scheme, Brahms paints *Le-ben* (life) as an appoggiatura gesture that will require a *crescendo* one beat before, and on *Le-* with a *diminuendo* to *-ben*, to allow it to be rhetorically heard throughout the dense chromatic setting.

The first *be-trüb-ten* (afflicted) presents several interpretive concerns: a) singing the half and whole steps in tune; b) signaling the off-beat *den* as an "expectation gesture" of what is to come: "to the afflicted"; and c) singing a momentary stress on *den* followed by a quick diminuendo prior to *be-*.[108] Throughout Brahms' setting of *(be)-trüb-(ten)*, beats 1 and 3 are also appoggiatura gestures that can be highlighted by brief stresses on each beat. At the same time we are expected to follow his instructions of crescendo that lasts for four beats from *Herzen* though *den betrübten.*

---

108 Brahms did not "have to write" these as off-beats; he also clarifies the same gesture at m.7 on "und" by which the same quick expressive elements can be applied.

Once the polyphonic, canon, 12-tone melody is presented we realize that at every four measures Brahms writes an added voice. Given already the analysis above, the clarity of the texture becomes more and more obscure. To prioritize the choices among the "conflicting goals" of attention to: intonation, balance, Brahms' dynamics, unwritten expressive marks, strong/weak syllabication, text consonant declamation in mm. 4–20 requires advanced preparation. Once the texture increases especially to three and four parts, our priorities throughout must be clarity of pitch and balancing (re-balance in many cases) gestures in each vocal line. Examples:

Measures 9–12: soprano (horizontal), alto and tenor (horizontal and vertical):

1. Soprano: intonation (-*trüb*-), diminished 5th (-*ten*), appoggiaturas (*den_be- trüb* with 8ve leap; "*Herr*" appoggiatura *gesture.*

2. Alto: Brahms' ⟨ ⟩ sung against sop; minor 6th leap, offbeat "*und*" appoggiatura *gesture* against sop; "*Le*" long appoggiatura *gesture* against soprano "*den*"; intonation *trüb*: b, a♯, a, g♯, a, g, with offbeat quick appoggiatura *gesture* on *den*, followed by "*trüb*" appoggiatura against soprano "*den.*"

3. Tenor: *Wa*- balance against S and A; 2nd note g against soprano f♯ (balance and pitch); tenor f♯ balance against soprano -*trüb*; f♯ to "c" *diminished 5th*; ½ steps tenor and soprano tune/balance against alto *den* offbeat appoggiatura gesture.

As above, the same "conflictual predicaments" occur in mm. 13–20, plus the added congestion of the bass part. Priorities throughout:

1. Practice singing each part with excellent melodic intonation; concentrate on wide leaps that demand accurate ear-voice

coordination; compared to tempered tuning, sing ascending half and whole steps *wide*, descending sing *narrow*.

2. Balance using Brahms' priorities: the high notes of each phrase reflect: a) an important stressed syllable; b) the expressive setting of *Mühseligen* (the miserable) with Brahms ⟣⟢, and *den betrübten Herzen* (to the bitter afflicted of heart) set by Brahms throughout warrant Brahms' priority of expression; allow them each to be heard.

3. Highlight the appoggiatura gestures, mentioned above to convey Brahms' musical and gestural rhetoric. If they conflict with his *written* dynamics expressions, they should be prioritized above the unwritten gestures.

4. On nearly every 1st and 3rd beat Brahms places the inherently stressed German syllables. These stresses will be easily accomplished if the conductor keeps track of the meaning of **C**: the natural pulse related to the half note. Because of the *langsam*, slow (tempo) indication, each measure will require the conductor to conduct in 4, with diluting somewhat the less important *weak* beats the 2 and 4, to allow the natural syllabic stresses on 1 and 3 to be heard.

5. Inevitably the stressed syllables, because of Brahms' setting will be a) found in a comparatively low texture, or b) Brahms written dynamics will take precedence; or c) an unwritten ⟣ ⟢ appoggiatura gesture may be more important to hear.

6. As the texture thickens, several stronger German consonants: **v** (**W**arum), **z** (Müh*s*eligen), **l** (**L**eben), **tr** (**tr**üb), **tz** (her*z*en) can be projected (though not exaggerated) to help aurally identify the text that is vertically obscured because of the thick texture. Depending on the context, the consonants: *m n l, ng, rr* can be momentarily sung by the choir.

Measures 20–26 conclude the opening section of *Warum*. The same priorities discussed previously apply to these measures. At the conclusion of m. 21 to the beginning of m. 23, carefully balance and tune the paired major and minor 10ths of the soprano/bass and alto/tenor duets. To balance vertically the SATB parts, the fast moving 8th notes can be best heard by allowing the tied half notes to decrease held-volume into the background. At m. 18, Brahms writes *f*, that applies to all SATB parts prior to the middle of m. 22 when he writes a long *diminuendo*. Balance vertically the SATB parts during the seven beats of mm. 21 and the first half of 22.

To create a well-balanced dynamic phrase at the diminuendo in mm. 22 to 24, place consecutively: *f mf mp p* and *pp* over the four half-notes, despite the biting harmonies C♯/D (alto/bass) on the downbeat, and B♭/A/F♯ on the third beat that can still be subtly etched out. Note the B♭ and G (bass/alto) create the expectation of a Phrygian cadence, but it is nullified by Brahms in m. 24 with a half cadence to A preceded by a suspension (E/D). Following this harmonically deceptive passage with Brahms' lovely diminuendo, the next entrance of "Wa" (of *Wa-rum*) seems purposely to shock (an "outrage") made vivid by Brahms' *f* marking. Brahms writes a *f* ⟩ *p* diminuendo in mm. 25–26 over six beats and given the brevity of the diminuendo, a *ritard* will seem quite natural. The second harmonic progression of V-I on "Wa-rum" beginning p requires a further diminuendo ("of acceptance") and certainly a ritard prior to the next new phrase.

Job 3:21, 22

Die des Todes warten und kommt nicht	Those who longs for death and it comes not,
Und gruben ihn wohl aus dem Verborgenen	and who dig well for it secretly,

Tuning, Balance, Choosing Priorities, mm. 28–54

Measures 28–43

Brahms sets four individual canons signifying "those," with imitative appoggiatura gestures "who long for death" with the lower three voices; these are followed by "and it comes not," with the adjective *dolce* accompanying the SATB 4-beat ⎯⎯. Brahms' *dolce* sign indicates not drama, but "acceptance;" the ⎯⎯ would be modest in this circumstance. While the *p* marks at m. 27 presumably continue, the possessive pronoun *Die des,* (those who [long for]), imitated in the lower three parts, deserve brief appoggiatura ⎯⎯ gestures to individually connect the *affect* of the verb *warten* (long for) to "those" providing "ownership. "Longing" juxtaposed to *kommt nicht* (it comes not) is made vivid by a series of diminished chords, especially the major 7th alto/bass dissonance **e/f** that symbolically calls for a phrygian cadence to e minor, but instead Brahms provides "disappointment" through the deceptive cadence to C major. The "disappointment symbolism" equates "death not coming to those who desire it" to depriving a "proper" progression to e minor, instead to C major.

Conductors, consider as an expressive aid for performance: over and over for seven mm. (33–39) Brahms writes "disappointment word-painting:" a) the upper three voices sing the *longing gesture, Die des Todes warten* including two appoggiaturas reinforcing *longing* with soprano/tenor in parallel 10ths; b) then Brahms writes a 14-beat crescendo, from *p* to *f* mm. 35–39; this 3½ measure crescendo occurs on *warten und kommt nicht* (it comes not); and c) it is repeated three times in the bass. Throughout the final three measures of this long phrase, Brahms melodically differentiates the soprano and bass in contrary motion, the tenor sings quick dotted-note gestures beginning with *und* (reinforced by the parallel range of the alto) leading to *kommt, kommt nicht, kommt nicht*. The end of the phrase on *nicht* is symbolically on C major; the soprano imitates (m. 38) the tenor of m. 37, reinforcing the crescendo to the *tutti nicht* followed by a quarter-note silence. This is a very dramatic gesture. It is a momentary gulp of realization of the depth of despair of words of the previous seven measures.

Measures 39–43 contain the final phrase of verse 21, *und grüben ihn wohl aus dem Verborgenen* (and who digs well for it secretly). These words follow the dramatic rest with a sudden loud cry *f* on a *unison* C. Each voice then descends to a low note: sopranos to E, altos to C#, tenors to A, and basses to A, which together form a comforting A major chord in closed position at m. 43. Brahms confirms the mood of the descending SATB parts with a *diminuendo* from mm. 42–43, ending with *p*. The descending gesture especially beginning at m. 41 with a series of passing eighth notes suggests a *diminuendo* that leads into Brahms' *diminuendo* (with a modest ritard) on the word "secretly."

Measures 43 – 54

Die sich fast freuen und sind fröhlich,	they nearly rejoice and are glad,
Das sie das Grab bekommen;	that they the grave have obtain;
Warum?	Why?

These words, "they nearly rejoice and are glad," in just four measures receive Brahms' special expressive marks: *espressivo,* ◁———▷, and are followed by *dolce* with a two-measure *diminuendo,* and a sudden *f* ▷— and a 3-beat rest. Why did Brahms write *espressivo,* ◁— ▷—, *p, dolce,* ▷— within eight measures? *Espressivo* relates to the words "they nearly rejoice and are glad," and reflects an anticipatory emotion climaxing in Brahms' ⟨ ⟩ on "are glad. " In this light Brahms' *espressivo* overlaps the four ascending SATB parts marked ⟨ ⟩ mm. 45–46, and the sudden high impact of the tenor voice; throughout all of these compositional nuances it would be hard to avoid *rubato*—a forward motion on this joyful four-measure phrase preceding the apex of Brahms' own crescendo on *fröhlich*. In this manner a quality of emotional exuberance will drive the tempo with forward motion from m. 43 to connect to Brahms' own exuberance marked ⟨ ⟩ in 45 to 46.

Dolce occurs on the final phrase of Job 3:22, "for they (who have hoped) the grave to have obtained." In this context, *dolce* and Brahms' *p* marks project a sweet melancholy meditation, amplified emotionally by Brahms' *diminuendo* on *bekommen* (obtained). Suddenly the "dream" is shattered by the unanticipated *f* on *War* ⟩ *p-um* . During the four *dolce* bars, the soprano and alto duet ascends on "that they, the grave" in parallel 3rd motion imitated initially by the tenor, and then by the bass. The ascending direction with the chromatic imitation inherently creates an expressive motion signaling a *crescendo* up to Brahms' diminuendo mark, that reinforces the emotion with the descending lines and series of suspensions leading to the final "(*bekom*)*-men*" cadence. Reinforce the *affect* of the *diminuendo* phrase, by allowing a natural ritard to occur as if coming to a rest; a diminuendo will enhance the impact of *f* at "Warum."

Job 3:23

Und dem Manne, des Weg
    verborgen ist,
Und Gott vor ihm denselben
    bedecked?
	and to men, whose way
	    is hidden
	and God from him himself has
	    hidden?

The text above is set by Brahms with a time change to 3/4. This is also a *tempo* change; under "time signature" three quarter notes are equal to two (prior) quarter notes, or a dotted half-note is equal to a prior half note. This time change is a 3 to 2 proportion, reflecting Brahms' years of study of Renaissance polyphony by which changes in *affect* were frequently expressed. The results of the proportional change mean that the final 30 measures are not only quicker but that the primary pulse is now related to a dotted half-note, i.e., one beat per bar. This new *affect* of mood provides less of a mournful spirit than Brahms' setting of his preceding 54 measures, and it also offers a comforting spirit for the transition to the text of the following 2nd movement: *Let us our heart with our hands lift up to God in heaven,* a sign of *comfort* by placing our trust in God and praising Him.

The text *Und dem Manne dass Weg verborgen ist* (and to men, whose way is hidden) is set to the same melody of the sopranos and tenors in parallel octaves at mm. 4–6, *Warum is das Licht gegeben dem Mühseligen* (Why is light given to those in misery). Brahms borrows that melody to retain and equate the spirit of the original first words to the similar *affect* of the final words: "and to men, whose way to the grave (and to God) is hidden." Brahms repeats the same questioning words in mm. 64–68 in which both the alto and bass voice repeat the imitation in a canon at the 4th. As a "law" this canon has been shifted to the primary pulse equal to one beat per bar. This quickening increases the rueful questioning of the words; this

mood can be expressed clearly with an unwritten crescendo to the high notes (D and A) of each phrase.

The second half of verse 23 of Job 3, *und Gott vor ihm denselben bedekket* (and from whom God has hidden himself), Brahms reflects by way of chromaticism and ascending lines with the longest crescendo of the motet hovering over nearly eight bars, the crying-out sorrow of humanities' loss of the grave, hidden ultimately by God. The emotional *affect* of Brahms' expressive writing confirms a momentary reminder that it is "God hiding himself" from man, that relates to the answer to the ultimate "why" (*Warum?*) question. This mood is dramatically pictured over the final eight measures of *f* ⟩⟩, repeated twice, with rests inserted between each word, signaling *outrage, sorrowful and inner acceptance.* Beginning m. 69, Brahms dramatically heightens the emotions of this text with continuous ascending and descending chromaticism of the vocal parts reinforced by vivid suspensions at 69, 70, 72, 74, 75) on five downbeats. *Topping it off*, like a final farewell of the final consequences, Brahms writes the longest continued crescendo that leads directly to the unanswered question: "Why": 3-measures *f* ⟩⟩ *p*; "Why" 4-measures *p* ⟩⟩ ?

The entire final section (54–84) of this motet suggests a *feeling* of ongoing *urgency and restlessness.* Brahms reinforces this *mood* with many compositional changes expressed by: 1) tempo change; 2) reintroduction of the soprano and alto melodies reminding us of the entire subject of part one: "questioning;" 3) quick ascending and descending chromatic vocal parts; 4) strong downbeat suspensions; 5) insertion of five *pp* or *p* marks, one *f* mark, and his highly direct marks ⟨⟨ ⟨⟨⟨ and ⟩⟩ ⟩⟩⟩ over 21 measures, hovering over more than two-thirds of these final 30 measures.

With the 27 marks Brahms has employed, he reinforces his harmony, melody, rhythm, texture, chromaticism and dissonances

that appear in nearly every bar. To bring clear aural meaning to this 30-measure compositional texture, a) follow in detail what Brahms has written; b) allow each phrase to confirm Brahms' gestures by modest application of "our own" ⤙⤚ imitating the ascending/descending motion of each line (mm. 54–58 and 64–69) and of the appoggiatura gestures; c) let the inherent two half-note-beats per measure be coupled with the pulse of the syllabic stresses; and d) relate Brahms' expressive (written and unwritten) gestures relate to *motion: employ rubato* with forward motion and slowing motion dovetailing the *emotion* of the text.

Be reminded throughout this final section by Brahms' comprehensive knowledge of Renaissance polyphony and proportional relationships, a 3:2 proportion (3 quarter notes are equal to 2 quarter notes) when he introduces $\frac{3}{4}$ time. The quicker tempo sets *urgently* the final verse of Job: "and to the man, whose way is hidden from God, and from whom God is hidden, Why?" Brahms' 84-measure repetition of the entire theme of the text progressively increases phrase by phrase the tension of the search to find the answer to "Why?"

Warum ist das Licht gegeben

Johannes Brahms op. 74 no. 1

2

BENJAMIN BRITTEN

THE EVENING PRIMROSE
FIVE FLOWER SONGS, OP. 47 NO. 4

Benjamin Britten (1913–1976) composed *Five Flower Songs* in 1950, on the occasion of the twenty-fifth wedding anniversary of Leonard and Dorothy Elmhirst, founders of the Dartington Hall project in progressive education and rural reconstruction. *The Evening Primrose*, on a poem by John Clare, is the slow movement of Britten's set of five songs with poems on the subject of flowers: 1) To Daffodils (Robert Herrick); 2) The Succession of the Four Sweet Months (Herrick); 3) Marsh Flowers (George Crabbe); 4) The Evening Primrose (John Clare); 5) Ballad of Green Broom (words anonymous).

It was in the fall of 1959 that I was introduced to Benjamin Britten's wonderful set of *Five Flower Songs* (published in 1951) when singing with the Chamber Singers at the University of California, Santa Barbara. The Chamber Singers were under the direction of Dorothy Westra, Professor of Voice at UCSB. Professor Westra introduced the Chamber Singers to the repertoire of many newly composed compositions (including Britten, Vaughan Williams, Irving Fine, and Aaron Copland) and the rich choral repertoire of the Renaissance ranging from Isaac, Senfl, and Josquin, to Palestrina, Lassus, and Byrd. In 1959–64, as an undergraduate at UCSB, little did I know how deeply influenced I would be by Dorothy Westra's choices of repertoire. More than fifty years later I continue to turn to choral music by these British, American, and Renaissance choral composers.

The Evening Primrose was my favorite of Britten's *Five Flower Songs*; it still is. The poem by John Clare provides an atmospheric setting of peacefulness—the primrose, a pale rose that blooms only at night. Clare sets his poignant description of the evening primrose in a series of seven rhymed couplets. The clear picture John Clare provides offers a series of events—a personalization of the life of the primrose. The first two couplets depict sunset and the *atmosphere* of dusk the primrose senses. Couplets 3 and 4 portray the initial blossoming followed by the "hermitlike" reaction to the yet-faded sun. The core of the unfolding primrose is couplet 5, followed by couplet 6—her continued night blooming with an awareness that day will soon rain down upon her pedals. In couplet 7 the sun appears, the primrose's gaze is (a)bashed (embarrassed), and her blossoms faint, wither, and are gone.

How might a choral conductor approach the score and anticipate performing this gem of a part-song? The primary catalyst for the director's interpretation of Britten's tastefully understated setting of this poignant poem is asking the question, "what compositional ingredients does Britten use to aurally present the subtle story of a night in the life of the primrose?" How can I aurally create with my choir the passing poetic emotions of *The Evening Primrose?* Specific feelings are aroused by the: a) general atmosphere, b) primrose unfolding, c) night blooming, unseen, d) primrose beauty, hidden by night, e) night blooming, (a)bashed in daylight, f) blooms wither, faint, gone.

OVERVIEW OF SPECIFIC TEXT/MUSIC
RELATIONSHIPS: PHRASES, SINGLE WORDS, MOODS

The picture of John Clare's textual images are imaginatively created by Britten's compositional technique through *change,* in *texture* (homophonic, polyphonic; duets, trios, quartets; backgrounds), *melody* (principal tune vertically set; imitative counterpoint and independent lines frequently answered in converse motion), *rhythm* (homophonic settings stressing natural strong/weak syllabification against the meter); Britten's stated mood: *Andante tranquillo;* range of dynamics— *ppp, pp, p, mf, f;* indications of crescendo and diminuendo; Britten's markings with accents and stresses on specific words and/or syllables; *dim.*

General Atmosphere: *Andante tranquillo* = "Walking (along) softly"influences performance:

a. Suggested tempo: quarter note = c. 58
b. Consistent rubato throughout: move with the stress/release of word syllabification
c. Phrase with the meaning/sense of word units–normally occur in 2-measure phrases.
d. *p* or *pp* is the background mood; Britten highlights changes with momentary ◁▷.
e. Of 31 bars, 21 measures are marked *p, pp, ppp*; keep poetic atmosphere in mind
f. Follow ◁ ▷; in soft contexts, these marks primarily mean *p* ◁ *mp* ▷ *p*
g. Mm. 14–15, Britten's first appearance of a longer cresc.; let results be equal to *mf*
h. Mm. 20–23 night full bloom, day appears; cresc to *f*; stress **Day** and o-pen eye
i. Poignant mm. 29–30: dim to *ppp*; m. 31 "gone" = 4-beats, *ppp* dimin. to niente

BRITTEN'S WORD/MUSIC RELATIONSHIPS
DETAILED ANALYSIS BENEATH RHYMED COUPLETS, WITH SUGGESTED INTERPRETIVE IDEAS

When once the sun sinks in the west,
And dewdrops pearl the evening's breast;

Measures 1–4

1. Two 2-measure phrases; motion and dynamic destinations: "sinks"; "pearl" and "eve"
   a. Triple note groups coincide with natural word stress: "When once, the sun, in the west"; "and dew-, drops pearl;" these "short/long" groups create long/short: "once the," "sinks in the"
   b. A♯/B dissonance = color for "pearl"; do not allow A♯/B to sound like a blurred octave; compared to tempered tuning, tune tenor A♯ slightly low in comparison to soprano B
2. Measures 2 and 4 final chords A and F♯ (restful); tune M3rds in each chord slightly low and balance.

Almost as pale as moonbeams are,
Or its companionable star,

The Evening Primrose
from Five Flower Songs

John Clare, 1835

Benjamin Britten
Op. 47, no. 4

Measures 5–7

"Triple groupings" reoccur in mm. 5–7: as long/short: Almost as/ pale as/moon beams. Sing "pale" and "moon" *mp+* in context of the *cresc.* In "Or its com-pan-ion": confirm the natural triple group arriving at "a" of "-ion-a" = *mp+* in this context. Sop: "pale," as an adjective and "moon" (of moon-beams) as the noun (subject) refers overall to the "sun"= 2nd subject that descends at dusk; *dim.* each phrase.

> The evening primrose opes anew
> Its delicate blossoms to the dew;

Measures 8–11

1. D♯ Major on "primrose" is a beautiful chord; allow a slight *cresc* into "prim-," tune carefully the D♯ (E♭) major chord on "prim-" highlighting this 3rd related progression. "The evening primrose opes" is sustained for 5+ beats; tune throughout these melting chords that present *primrose,* the subject of the poem, on the 3rd related progression F♯ to D♯.

2. "anew" B7 Major chord—first appearance of this color-chord highlighting "anew;" bass B and soprano A♯ must be balanced and be carefully tuned.

3. Tenor: "its delicate blossoms to the dew" = a single voice; SAB *ppp* "its blossoms" is an "impressionistic reminder" of the primrose budding; observe *ppp* background.

> And, hermit-like, shunning the light,
> Wastes its fair bloom upon the night,

Measures 12–15

1. "hermitlike, shunning the light"—word-painting texture = *closed/dense;* harmony: 8 chords all dissonant; alto is "half-step shuttle" 8 repetitions. Balance all SATB chords; tune carefully M7th chords; observe "shun" stress mark. Phrasing should follow the punctuation: And, her-mit-like, shun-ning the light.

> Who, blindfold to its fond caresses,
> Knows not the beauty he possesses.

Measures 16–19

1. "Who, blindfold to its fond caresses"—note SAB imitation; "Who" = "We" miss blooming; we are "blindfolded" by night.
2. Bass imitates descending soprano and alto: A, F♯, D, B cascade, meaning at night we all do "Know not the beauty, he (primrose) possesses."
3. And we do not feel "caresses" (soprano, alto duet); bass confirms we "know not the beauty." Britten's very deliberate *pp* $\longleftarrow\longrightarrow$ emphasizes we *all* miss the "fond caresses" and "beauty" the primrose possesses.

> Thus it blooms on while night is by;
> When day looks out with open eye,

Measures 20–23

1. "Thus it blooms on while night is by; When day looks out with open eye"—this phrase contains the most dramatic gesture of the whole piece: from *pp*, Britten writes *cresc.* from "Thus" to "When day;" *f* on "When"; *accent* on "day"; "looks out with" $\longrightarrow$ to *accent* on "o" of "open"; "- pen eye" = *diminuendo*. Follow Britten's explicit dynamics and accents.
2. In these 4 measures the bass is "static" on F♯ (8 beats), and octave Bs (8 beats) representing a dramatic connection: "blooming at night" followed by "day opening eyes."
3. Tenor sings primarily half or whole steps for 16 beats; alto half steps for seven beats; tune carefully throughout
4. Suddenly, "day" and "o" are punctuated by soprano and

alto leaps; on "o" the soprano D♯ slams against the tenor E, and the alto sings A♯ against the bass B. Both M7 dissonances occur simultaneously; Britten is drawing attention to the "sudden occurrence of day."

> 'Bashed at the gaze it cannot shun,
> It faints and withers and is gone.

Measures 24–25

1. The appearance of the "open eyes of day" leads to "'Bashed at the gaze it cannot shun," for which Britten writes *p* dim ; this is a surprisingly muted 2-measure reaction to the drama of the prior to measures that contain *f* dynamics, two accents, and sudden dynamic changes.

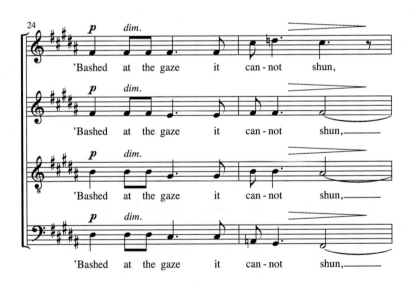

Measures 26–31

2. Six measures provide a "remembrance" of what happens

to the primrose during day: *It faints and withers and is gone*. These tender words Britten spreads over 6 measures of imitative polyphony: S and T; A and B (mm. 26–29), concluding in final 2 measures—slower rhythms begin at m. 31; final chord on open F♯–C♯ are "non-committal" harmonically. The "open" chord reminds us of the emotional connection to the whole story. The primrose always fades during day and faints and withers. Irony—we can only notice the beauty at night; difficult to see. The primrose will always enjoy a rich life of delicate blossoms of beauty that caresses every night.

—APPENDIX B—

MOODS SUGGESTED BY CHORD PROGRESSIONS AND VOICING

Chord progressions and choices of voicing can suggest dynamic nuances that might not already be indicated in the score. Here are some examples to demonstrate how to interpret some chord progressions in expressive ways. Play them several times to hear their affect, their mood; feel the emotion.

For example, I ii IV I implies *diminuendo* to ii, *crescendo* to IV, and *diminuendo* to I. Note: In many examples, a major chord followed by a minor chord suggests *diminuendo*, and a minor chord followed by a major chord suggests the opposite: *crescendo*. Of course there are variants; some progressions seem "equal" and may not suggest any particular dynamic change.

Another important series of chords is shown here. Play the same chord with varied high notes in the soprano part, taking care not to double the high note with the 3rd or 5th in the soprano. Play an A major chord with the A in the soprano; repeat, but put the C# in the soprano; then play the same with an E in the soprano. These three textures create mood changes: The root suggests "the end, and final resolve"; the third suggests "the emotion may not be resolved—it's not solved"; the fifth suggests "ongoing, ever present, a truth."

Play chords with the root in the bass, then the third in the bass, then the fifth in the bass. Root has a sense of permanence; the third is not permanent and is possibly ongoing; the fifth is not stable but suggests suggests on-going eternity.

Chords: *Bass Positions and Soprano Positions = Moods*

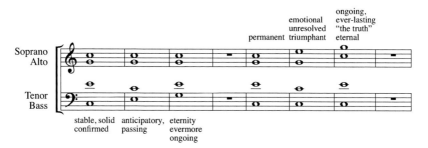

Chord Progressions create moods.

Moods imply dynamics; *dynamics depend on vocal direction.*
Most major to minor chords = *dim;* minor to major = *cresc.*

—APPENDIX C—

Harvard Glee Club
Jameson Marvin, Conductor 1978–2010
† edited by Jameson Marvin for the Harvard Glee Club
* published edition by Jameson Marvin
‡ commissioned by or written for the Harvard Glee Club
♦ for men's chorus and orchestra

Renaissance

Agricola, Alexander	† Credo Je ne vis oncques*
Alonso	† La tricotea
Anonymous	Ave regina caelorum
	† Dolent depart*
	† Rex autem David*
Anonymous chants	Adoro te devote
	Alma redemptoris mater
	Puer natus
	Salve Regina
	Veni Emmanuel (arr. A. T. Davison)
Brumel, Antoine	† Du tout plonget*
	Tous les regretz
Byrd, William	Jesu nostra redemptio
	† Non nobis Domine (Dona nobis pacem)
	Non vos relinquam orphanos
	Mass for 3 Voices —Sanctus

	Short Communion Service —
	Agnus Dei
Certon, Pierre	Que n'est elle aupres de may
Compère, Loyset	† Tous les regretz
Cornysh, William	A Robyn, gentil Robyn
DeBussy, Vincent	Las il n'a nul mal
Desprez, Josquin	† Absalon fili mi*
	Déploration sur la mort
	d'Ockeghem
	Ecce, tu pulchra es
	Missa Mater patris
	† Kyrie*
	† Gloria*
	† Agnus Dei
	Missa Sine Nomine
	† Kyrie
	† Agnus Dei
	† *Missa La sol fa re mi* —Sanctus
	† El grillo
	Si j'ay perdu mon ami
	Tu pauperum refugium
	† Tu solus, qui facis mirabilia*
Dufay, Guillaume	† *Missa Ave Regina coelorum* —
	Agnus Dei
	Anima mea liquefacta est
Dunstable, John	Kyrie (*a single movement*)
Ensino, Juan del	† Mi libertad en sosiego
Ferrabosco, Alphonso I	† Vocem meam audisti
Ferrabosco, Alphonso II	Lamentations of Jeremiah
Gastoldi, Giovanni	Tutti venite armati
	Viver lieto voglio
Genet, Elzéar	Alma redemptoris mater
	Regina coeli
	Virgo prudentissima
Gombert, Nicholas	† O gloriosa Domina*
Handl, Jacob	Ante luciferum
	† Ascendit Deus*

	De coelo veniet
	Haec est dies
	O beata Trinitas
	Pueri, concinite
Hassler, Hans Leo	Cantate Domino
	Laetentur coeli
Hildegard von Bingen	Caritas abundant
Isaac, Heinrich	† Quis dabit capite meo aquam
Lassus, Orlando	† La nuict froide
	Matona, mia cara
Morley, Thomas	Say, Dear, will you not have me?
Ockeghem, Johannes	† *Missa Mi-Mi*—Agnus Dei
	Intemerata Dei Mater
Palestrina, Giovanni P.	† Sicut cervus desiderat
Praetorius, Michael	Lo, how a rose (arr. A. T. Davison)
Rue, Pierre de la	† *Missa Conceptio tuo* —Kyrie
	Missa pro Defunctis (*excerpts*)
†	Porquoy non
Ruffo, Vincenzo	*Missa sine nomine* —Sanctus
Senfl, Ludwig	† Quis dabit oculis
Shepherd, John	Alleluia/Confitemini Domino
Tallis, Thomas	If ye love me
	Lamentations of Jeremiah
	† *Mass for 4 Voices* —Sanctus*
	† Agnus Dei
	This is my commandment
Taverner, John	† Magnificat*
Tinctoris, Johannes	† *Mass for 3 Voices* —Kyrie
Tomkins, Thomas	O Lord how manifold are Thy works
	The heavens declare the glory of God
	When David Heard
Vecchi, Orazio	† Quando penso
	† Imitatione del Venetiano*
Viadana, Lodovico	† Non turbetur cor vestrum*
Victoria, Tomás Luis de	O regem omnes
	O vos omnes

Weelkes, Thomas	Come sirrah Jack ho
	How late is my rash
White, Robert	Regina coeli

Baroque

Monteverdi, Claudio	† Lamento della Ninfa:
	Non havea febo
	Amor
	Sì tra sdegnosi
Purcell, Henry	Catches:
	Barthlomew Fair
	I gave her cakes
	Once, twice, thrice, I Julia tried
	Glees:
	Ah, how gladly we Believe
	He that drinks is immortal
Schütz, Heinrich	◆ An den Wassern zu Babel
	Gib unsern Fürsten
	O quam tu pulchra es, amica mea

Classic & Romantic
◆ *for men's chorus and orchestra*

Anonymous (Spanish)	El Padre nuestro
Beethoven, Ludwig van	Prisoners Chorus from *Fidelio*
Berlioz, Hector	Finale to Part II from *Damnation of Faust*
Brahms, Johannes	Ich schwing' mein Horn
	◆ Alto Rhapsodie
Bruckner, Anton	Inveni David
Cocchi, Giocchino	Bacchanal
D'Indy, Vincent	Les trois habillements
	Printemps nouveau
Flagg, Josiah	Halleluia
Haydn, Franz Joseph	Alles hat sein Zeit
Haydn, Michael	Abschiedlied
Jones, G. H.	Deus salutis (arr. Mansel Thomas)

Liszt, Franz	Psalm 116
Mendelssohn, Felix	Beati mortui
	Im Süden
	Trinklied
Moussorgsky, Modest	Podnimaisia, molodtsi from *Khovanshchina*
Offenbach, Jacques	Drig, Drig, Drig from *Tales of Hoffmann*
Purcell, Henry	He that drinks is immortal
Reger, Max	Liebchens Bote
	Hochsommernacht
	Ich hab' die Nacht geträumet
Schubert, Franz	Der Geistertanz
	Die Nacht
	◆ Gesang der Geister über den Wassern
	Gott meine Zuversicht (Psalm 23)
	Grab und Mond
	La Pastorella
	Mondenschein
	Nachtgesang im Walde
	Nachthelle
	Sehnsucht
	Ständchen
	Widerspruch
Schumann, Robert	◆ Die Rose stand im Tau
	Zigeunerlied
Sibelius, Jean	Natus in curas
Strauss, Richard	Traumlicht
Wagner, Richard	Pilgrim's Chorus from *Tannhauser*
	Sailors' Chorus from *The Flying Dutchman*
Webbe, Samuel	Glorious Apollo (arr. A. T. Davison)
Weber, Carl Maria von	Huntsmen's Chorus from *Der Freischütz*
Weber, Gottfried	Gebet

White, Benjamin Franklin	Power (early American)
Zelter, Carl Friedrich	Dreistigkeit

Eastern European

Anonymous (Georgian)	Dachrilis Simghera
	† Shen khar venakhi*
	† Voi di vo*
	† Gazapkhuli*
Bartók, Béla	Five Slovak Folk Songs
Chesnokov, Pavel	Spaseniye sodelal
Dvořák, Antonín	Tri Muzské Sbory, Op. 43:
	Zal
	Divná voda
	Devce v háji
	Five Songs for Men's Voices:
	Prípoved' lásky
	Hostina
	Liebeslied im Garten
Gliere, Reyngol'd	Poslanie u Sibir'
Gretchaninoff, Alexandre	Slava...Yedinorodniy Sine
Ippolitov-Ivanov, Mikhail	Psalm 132
Janáček, Leos	Ani tak nesvite
	Láska opravdivá
	Ó lásko
	Stava plakava
	Vínek Stonulý
Jenö, Ádám	Falu vegen kurta kocsma
Kastalsky, Alexander	S nami Bog
Kodály, Zoltán	Esti dal
	Fölszallot a pava
	Hej bungözsdi bandi
	Huszt
	Jelige
	Mulato gajd
	Rabhazanak fia
Novikov, Anatoly	Doroghi
Rachmaninoff, Sergei	The All-Night Vigil:

	Slava v vishnih Bogu
	Bogoroditse devo
	Shestopsalmiye
Stravinsky, Igor	Four Russian Peasant Songs:
	U spasa v' Chigisakh
	Ovsen
	Shchuka
	Puzishche
Suchon, Eugen	Slovenska l'udova piesen:
	Co sa stalo nove
	Ej dziny dziny dom
	Tam medzi horami
Sulyok, Imre	Alkony
	Est
Vartabed, Gomidas	*Holy Mass of the Armenian Church* —Sanctus

Contemporary

Alfvén, Hugo	Stemning
Albrecht, Maximillian	Exultet Sanctus
Argento, Dominick	‡ Apollo in Cambridge: A Harvard Triptych
	The Shepherd of King Admetus
	The Voiceless
	Fata Morgana
	• The Revelation of Saint John the Divine
Baksa, Robert	Pursuing the horizon
Barber, Samuel	A Stopwatch and an Ordnance Map
Barnett, Carol	‡ One Equal Music
Bernstein, Leonard	Almighty Father
	‡ Dedication
	‡ Lonely Men of Harvard
Beveridge, Thomas	‡ Drop, drop, slow tears*
	‡ I seek the present time
Biebl, Franz	Ave Maria

Binkerd, Gordon	‡ Ay waukin O*
Boursy, Richard	‡ The house was quiet and the world was calm
Brewer, Herbert	Alexander
Britten, Benjamin	The Ballad of Little Musgrave and Lady Barnard
Carter, Elliot	‡ Emblems
	‡ Tarantella*
Chatman, Steven	Reconciliation
Conte, David	Canticle
Copland, Aaron	The Boatman's Dance (arr. Irving Fine)
	Simple Gifts (arr. Irving Fine)
Cowell, Henry	Evensong at Brookside
	Luther's Carol for his Son
Distler, Hugo	Lied eines Verliebten
Elkies, Noam	‡ Al-Na Tomar
	‡ Mi Y'malel Gvurot Yisrael
	‡ Ma'oz Tzur
	‡ Saleinu 'Al Kteifeinu
Ellingboe, Bradley	‡ Innisfree
Ferko, Frank	‡ O coruscans lux stellarum*
Fine, Irving	‡ McCord's Menagerie:*
	Vulture Gryphus
	Jerboa
	Mole
	Clam
	‡ Pianola D'Amore*
Floyd, Carlisle	Death Came Knocking
Fussell, Charles	‡ A Walt Whitman Sampler*
Gibbs, Armstrong	She Walks in Beauty
Glick, Aul Irving	Yoshev B'seter
Gomidas	Sanctus
Gustafsson, Kaj-Erik	*Missa a cappella* —Agnus Dei
	Ave Maria
	Salve Regina
Harbison, John	‡ Nunc dimittis*
Heath, Fenno	The Lamb

Heiler, Anton	Assumpta est
Hindemith, Paul	Das verfluchte Geld
	Demon of the Gibbet
	Der Tod
	Erster Schnee
	Birthday Canon
Hoddinott, Alan	Four Welsh Songs:
	Croen Y Dfafad Felen
	Breuddwyd Y Bardd
	Lisa Lan
	Dadl Dau
Holst, Gustav	‡ Before Sleep
Hulse, Brian	‡ Stabat Mater
Ives, Charles	A Christmas Carol
	Circus Band
	Serenity
Jeffers, Ronald	Solitude
Jersild, Jörgen	Guldsmed
Lauridsen, Morten	‡ Ave dulcissima Maria
Lister, Rodney	‡ The Oxen*
Lundvik, Hildor	Höst
Madetoja, Leevi	De profundis
Marvin, Jameson	‡ Cantantes Licet Usque Eamus
Mechem, Kirke	Blow Ye the Trumpet
Milhaud, Darius	‡ Psaume 121*
Moravec, Paul	‡ Credo
Morris, Stephen	Dona nobis pacem
	Four long hours
Nelson, Paul	A Lullaby
O'Regan, Tarik	‡ Se lamentar augelli*
Orff, Carl	In taberna from *Carmina Burana*
Pärt, Arvo	De profundis
Paulus, Steven	‡ Shall I compare Thee?
Poos, Heinrich	Zeichen am Weg
	Ein jegliches hat seine Zeit
	In der frühe

Poulenc, Francis	‡ Chanson à boire*
	La belle si nous étions
	Laudes de Saint Antoine de Padoue
	Quatre Petites Prières de Saint
	François d'Assise
Rasmussen, Kirstina	‡ Little Man*
Roberton, Hugh	The Cloths of Heaven
Sametz, Steven	‡ Dulcis Amor*
Sandström, Sven-David	*Tre Stycken for Manskor* —Kyrie
Schickele, Peter	‡ A Veritable Paean of Praise*
Schönberg, Arnold	Der Deutsche Michael
	♦ Survivor from Warsaw
	Verbundenheit
Stravinsky, Igor	♦ Oedipus Rex
Tavener, John	‡ Awed by the Beauty*
Thompson, Randall	Quis multa gracilis
	Frostiana:
	Stopping by Woods on a
	Snowy Evening
	The Pasture
	‡ Tarantella*
Thomson, Virgil	‡ Cantantes eamus*
Vaughan Williams, Ralph	*Five Mystical Songs*–Antiphon
	Sir John in Love–Drinking Song
	Epitaph on John Jaybeard of Diss
Warrell, Arthur	In Saint Paul's
Washburn, Jon	Three Shakespearean Songs
Washburn, Robert	O Mistress Mine
Werdin, Eberhard	Zwei Trinklieder:
	Der edelste Brunnen
	Der Buhle im Keller
Weill, Kurt	♦ Das Berliner Requiem
Willan, Healey	The Agincourt Song
	Missa Brevis —Kyrie and Gloria
Yannatos, James	‡ Buffalo Bill*
	♦ Symphony No. 2
	Four Sillies
	Prais'd be the Fathomless

Universe
‡ Out of the Earth I Sing
‡ The Family of Mankind
Zytowski, Carl   Bogurodzica

Folksongs
Arrangements, if not otherwise indicated
‡ arranged for the Harvard Glee Club
† edited by Jameson Marvin for the Harvard Glee Club

Allaway, Ben   I'm a-comin'
Anonymous   Five Mountain Songs
Bartholomew, Marshall   Shenandoah
Davison, Archibald T.   ‡ The Foggy Dew
                                  ‡ Sacramento
                                  ‡ Shenandoah
                                  ‡ Spanish Ladies
Dawson, William   Ain'a That Good News?
                                  Ev'ry Time I Feel the Spirit
                                  There is a Balm in Gilead
Elkies, Noam   ‡ When Johnny Comes
                                       Marching Home
                                  ‡ The Salley Gardens
                                  ‡ Huan hsi i jia (Taiwanese)
                                  ‡ It Came Upon a Midnight Clear
                                  ‡ We Three Kings
Forbes, Elliot   ‡ K'ang Ting Love Song* (Chinese)
                                  ‡ Arirang* (Korean)
(Stephen Foster)   ‡ Deep River
(Stephen Foster)   ‡ Old Folks at Home
Foster—Jenkins, J. W.   Laura Lee
Foster—Shaw, Robert/
   Parker, Alice   Gentle Annie
Foster—Vaughan Williams,
   Ralph   Old Folks at Home
Hairston, Jester   Poor man Lazrus
Heath, Fenno   Sometimes I Feel Like a
                                       Motherless Child

	Er is een kindetje (Swedish)
Holst, Gustav	Swansea Town
	‡ I Love my Love (British)
Ishii, K.	Hamachidori Bushi (Japanese)
Jeffers, Ron	Waitin for the Dawn of Peace
	Tentin' Tonight
Keller, Mark	Pretty Saro
Kreger, Bernard	Were you there?
Leong, Kevin ed.	‡ New Britain
Marvin, Jameson ed.	† Gazapkhuli* (Georgian)
	† Voi di vo* (Georgian)
	‡ Sora n Bushi (Y. Fukunaga)
	(Japanese)
	‡ All Through the Night*
	‡ Riders in the Sky
	‡ Shenandoah*
	‡ Barb'ra Allen* (British)
	‡ Danny Boy* (Irish)
	‡ Greensleeves* (British)
	‡ I Love my Love* (British)
	‡ The Minstrel Boy*
	‡ Sky Boat Song* (Chinese)
	‡ Flower Drum Song* (Chinese)
	‡ K'ang Ting Love Song* (Chinese)
	‡ Shen khar venakhi* (Georgian)
	(Shimizu, Osamu)
	† Mogami Gawa Funa Uta
	(Japanese)
Mich'evich, Denis	Ax Ty St'Ep' (Russian)
(Paliashvili, Zakhary)	
Pedrotti, Antonio	La Banda from *Five Italian*
	Mountain Songs (Italian)
Roberton, Hugh	My luve is like a red, red rose
	(British)
Sametz, Steven	‡ Kas tieh todi
	‡ Ne sedi, Djemo
	Pai dul l'i V'ydul Ya

Santos, Rosendo	‡ Sampaguita from *Two Philippine Folk Songs* (Filipino)
Sells, Robert	Joshua
Shaw, Robert/Parker, Alice	Laura Lee
	Lowlands
	Swansea Town
	What shall we do with the drunken sailor?
	L'amour de moy (French)
	Viva L'amour (French)
	Al olivo (Spanish)
Underwood, Samuel	My love's an arbutus (British)
Urquhart, Peter (J Green)	‡ Body and Soul
	‡ Kiso Bushi (Japanese)
	‡ Tosa Bushi (Japanese)
Wiliford, Vance	Suo gân (Welsh)
Vaughan Williams, Ralph	Bushes and Briars (British)
	Down among the dead men (British)
	Linden Lea (British)
	Loch Lomond (Scotish)
	The Seeds of Love (British)
	The Turtle Dove (British)
	Ward the Pirate (British)
Warrell, Arthur	Will ye no come back again? (British)
Williford, Lawrence	Suo Gân

Radcliffe Choral Society
Beverly Taylor, Conductor 1978-1995
Jameson Marvin, Conductor 1995-2010
+*edited by Jameson Marvin for RCS*
*published edition

Renaissance

British, 13th century	Hodie Christus natus est, Alleluya
	Ther is no rose of swych vertu
Spanish, mid 13th century	Cantigas de Santa Maria,
	Cunctisimus from *Llibre Vermell*
Late 13th century	Alleluia-Psallat from *Worcester fragments*
14th century chant	Angelus ad Virginem
Animuccia, Giovanni	Lodate Dio
Byrd, William	+ Haec dies
	+ Non nobis domine (Dona nobis pacem)
	O Gloriosa Domina
	+ Sacerdotes Domini
Busnois, Antoine	+ A vous sans aultre
Caccini, Francesca	Aure volanti
Calvisius, Sethus	Musik und Gesang
Constantini, Alessandro	Confitemini Domino
Dering, Richard	Quem vidistis pastores
Desprez, Josquin	+ Ave verum corpus
	In te Domine speravi
	+ Recordare
Donati, Ignazio	Non vos relinquam orphanos
Dufay, Guillaume	* Alma redemptoris Mater II
	+ Aures ad nostras deitatis preces
	Flos florum
Dunstable, John	* Quam pulchra es
	+ Alma redemptoris Mater
Grenot	Nova vobis gaudia
Guerrero, Francisco	A un niño llorando

Handl, Jacob	+ Pueri concinite
	Regnum mundi
	Trahe me post te
	Virgines prudentes
Hildegard von Bingen	O rubor sanguine
	Caritas abundat
	In evangelium
Janequin, Clement	Ce moys de may
Lassus, Orlando	Fulgebunt justi
	* In pace
Monteverdi, Claudio	* Three Canzonets:
	Io mi vivea
	Sì come crescon
	Hor care canzonette
	Godi pur del bel sen
	Scherzi Musicali
	+ Venite, venite
Morales, Cristóbal de	O magnum mysterium
Morley, Thomas	This love is but a wanton fit
	Though Philomena lost her love
Ockeghem, Johannes	+ *Missa Sine Nomine* —Kyrie,
	Sanctus
	+ *Missa Cuiusvis toni* —Gloria
	Ave maris stella
Palestrina, Giovanni Pierluigi	+ *Missa Sine Nomine* —Benedictus
	+ Pueri hebraeorum
	* Hodie Christus natus est
	+ *Missa O admirabile commercium*
	—Sanctus
	* Magnificat
Praetorius, Michael	+ In dulci jubilo
	+ Allein Gott in der Höh sei dir
	Ecce Maria genuit
Staden, Johann	+ Das Leid ist hier
Sweelinck, Jan Pieter	Or sus, serviteurs du Seigneur
Tallis, Thomas	*Mass for 3 Voices* —Sanctus
	+ Sancte Deus
Taverner, John	* Gloria in Excelsis

	+ Audivi coeli
	Ave regina coelorum
Vecchi, Orazio	Fammi una canzonetta capricciosa
Viadana, Ludovico	Jubilate Deo
Victoria, Tomás Luis da	+ Duo seraphim clamabant (ed. Kevin Leong)
	Tenebrae factae sunt
	* Una hora
Weelkes, Thomas	Four arms, two necks, one wreathing
	Cease, sorrows, now
	Come sirrah Jack ho!
	The Nightingale
	Strike it up, Tabor
Wilbye, John	Come shepherd swains

Baroque
* for orchestra and women's chorus

Bach, Johann Sebastian	Suscepit Israel from *Magnificat*
Charpentier, Marc-Antoine	Antienne a la Vièrge (Regina coeli)
Couperin, François	Troisième Leçon de Ténébres
Galuppi, Baldassare	+ Dixit Dominus (Psalm 110)
Hammerschmidt, Andreas	Herzlich Lieb had ich dich
	Lobe den Herren, meinen Seele
Hasse, Johann Adolf	* Miserere in C Minor (Psalm 51)
Lotti, Antonio	Sanctus
Pergolesi, Giovanni	* Stabat Mater
Porpora, Niccoló	Magnificat
Schein, Johann Hermann	Lobet Gott, ihr Christen allzugleich
Schütz, Heinrich	Anima mea liquefacta est
	Adjuro vos, filiae Jerusalem
	Was betrübst du dich, meine Seele

Classic and Romantic
* for orchestra and women's chorus

Bizet, George	Dans l'air nous suivons des yeux la fumée from *Carmen*
Brahms, Johannes	Drei geistliche Chöre, op. 37 O bone Jesu Adoramus te Regina coeli Vier Gesänge für Frauenchor with horn and harp, op. 17 Nun stehn die Rosen in Blüte Psalm 13 * Ave Maria Klänge, from Fünf Duette, op. 66
Chesnokov, Pavel	Dostoyno yest' Milost mira
Crotch, William	Comfort, O Lord, the soul of thy servant
Daniels, Mabel	Dum Diana vitrae
Debussy, Claude	Salut printemps
Haydn, Michael	Anima nostra * *Missa St. Aloysii*
Ibert, Jacques	Les fleurs des champs
Ippolitov-Ivanov, Mikhail	Heruvimskaya pesn'
Mendelssohn, Felix	Surrexit pastor bonus Laudate Domino Laudate pueri Dominum
Nicolai, Otto	Elfen, weiss, from *The Merry Wives of Windsor*
Reger, Max	Drei Gesänge, op. 111B Er ist's Im Himmelrich ein Haus steht
Rheinberger, Josef	Ave Maris Stella
Schubert, Franz	Ständchen Valses Nobles
Schumann, Robert	Die Capelle

	Soldenbraut
	Ländliches Lied, op. 29 no. 2
	Meerfey
	Der Wasserman
	In Meeres Mitten
Verdi, Giuseppe	Lauda a la Vergine Maria
	S'allontanarono from *Macbeth*
	La sorelle vagabonde from *Macbeth*
Voynich, E. L.	Our Lady sings

Contemporary
* for orchestra and women's chorus
‡ commissioned by or written for RCS

Andemicael, Awet	‡ Spring, the Sweet Spring
Bárdos, Lajos	Cantemus
	Magos a Rutafa:
	Heves lendülettel
	Igen ritmikusan
	Scherzando
Bacon, Ernst	Precepts of Angelus Selesius
Balassa, Sándor	Bánatomtól szabadulnék
Barber, Samuel	Heaven-Haven, A Nun Takes the Veil
Bartók, Béla	Five Hungarian Folk Songs
	18 Part Songs for Women's Voices:
	Bánat
	Héjja, héjja, karahéjja!
	Keserves
	Legénycsúfoló
	Jószág-igéző
	Játék
	Ne láttalak volna!
	Elment a madárka
Béobide, José Maria	Tantum ergo
Bialosky, Marshall	Seven Academic Graffiti

Bloch, Ernest	Silent Devotion Response from *Sacred Service*
Bridge, Frank	Peter Piper
Britten, Benjamin	Ceremony of Carols
	Missa Brevis
Bullard, Alan	Sursum corda
Caplet, André	*Messe à trois voix*
	O Salutaris Hostia
Carter, Elliott	* The Harmony of Morning
Casals, Pablo	Eucaristica
	Nigra sum
Chihara, Paul	Magnificat
Clarke, Henry Leland	The bounty of Athena
Copland, Aaron	The House on the Hill
	An Immortality
	At the River (arr.)
	Ching-a-ring Chaw (arr.)
	Long time ago (arr.)
	Zion's Walls (adapt.)
Damase, Jean-Michel	Sicilienne Variée
Daniels, Mabel	‡ Dum Diana vitrea
Davis, Betsy Warren	‡ The apple tree madrigals
DeBraal, Andries	An immorality
	Regina caeli
Debussy, Claude	* Sirènes from *Nocturnes*
Defotis, William	How Many Times...
Dello Joio, Norman	Regina caeli
	A jubilant song
Diamond, David	All in green went my love riding
	The glory is fallen out of the sky
Dienes, Katherine	Ave verum corpus
Distler, Hugo	Der Jahrkreis, op. 5
	Bei stiller Nacht
	Gott ist unsre Zuversicht
	O Heiland, reiss die Himmel auf
	Jesus Christus, gestern und heute
	Lied vom Winde

Duruflé, Maurice	Tota pulchra es
Duson, Dede	And back again
Elkies, Noam	The Salley Gardens
Fauré, Gabriel	Tantum ergo
Fine, Irving	The White Knight's Song from *Three Choral Settings from Alice in Wonderland*
Goemanne, Noel	*Missa Hosanna*
Heiller, Anton	O Kind, o wahrer Gottessohn
Heiss, John	Three Songs from Sandberg
Holland, Jonathan	A Visit to St. Elizabeth's
Holst, Gustav	Ave Maria
	* Seven Part Songs for Female Voices and Strings, op. 44
	Choral Hymns from the Rig Veda, Groups II, III
Honegger, Arthur	* Cantique de Pâques
Hovhaness, Alan	Fuji
Hovland, Egil	Laudate Dominum
Hurd, Michael	Five Epitaphs from an Imaginary Graveyard
	Missa Brevis
Ives, Charles	A Christmas Carol
	Cradle Song
Ives, Grayston	‡ Five sacred songs
	Infant holy, infant lowly (Polish, arr.)
Johnson, James	‡ Hodie Christus natus est
	‡ How they brought good news by sea
Jordorkovsky, Daniela	‡ Song
Kankainen, Jukka	Sävel
	Kesäyö
Kastalsky, Alexander	Milost' mira
	Miloserdiya dveri
	Liturgy of St. John Chrysostom
Kidd, Richard	Wind-Song
Kocsár, Miklós	Libera me

	Missa in A—Sanctus, Agnus Dei
Kodály, Zoltán	Esti dal
	Hegyi Éjszakák (Mountain Nights)
	Négy Olasz from Three Madrigals
	Wainimoinen Makes Music
	The Angels and the Shepherds
Kretschmar, Gunther	Jauchzet dem Herrn
Kyr, Robert	Toward Eternity
Langlais, Jean	Chant Litanique
	Tantum ergo
Larson, Libby	If I can stop one heart from breaking
Lekberg, Sven	Let all the world in every corner sing
Loeffler, Charles M.	By the Rivers of Babylon
Lukáš, Zdeněk	Kvardyan
Martinů, Bohuslav	Narození Páne
Mellnäs, Arne	Aglepta
McRae, Shirley	Love's Music
Micheelson, Hans	Mit Fried und Freud ich fahr dahin
Moravec, Vincent Paul	i thank You God (e. e. cummings)
Ness, Patricia van	Nos sumus custodes Angeli
Nowak, Lionel	Love's lesson
	Wisdom exalteth her children
Nystedt, Knut	Hosanna
Karlekens Lov	Seek ye the Lord
O'Regan, Tarik	Columba aspexit
Paulus, Stephen	Love letters (1980)
	Cats, friends and lovers
Paynter, John	There is no rose
Perera, Ronald	Earthsongs
Persichetti, Vincent	Love
Pinkham, Daniel	An Emily Dickinson Mosaic
	In youth is pleasure
Poulenc, Francis	Ave verum corpus

	Litanies à la Vièrge noire
	Petites voix
Qualliotine, Armand	if
	in time of daffodils
Rachmaninoff, Sergei	Six Choruses, Women's Chorus & Piano
	Ñevólia (Captivity)
	Vespers (excerpts)
Riegger, Wallingford	Evil shall not prevail
Russell, Carlton T.	A Psalm Mosaic
Schickele, Peter	Three Meditations
Schmitt, Florent	En Bonnes Voix, op. 91
	La mort du rossignol
Schuman, William	* Concert on old English rounds
Sköld, Agneta	*Missa Brevi*—Kyrie, Gloria
Solomon, Leah	Yihyu L'ratzon
Starer, Robert	Come sleep
Stravinsky, Igor	* Cantata
	* Four Russian Peasant Songs for Equal Voices
Scoboda, Upravil	Okolo Bludova
Tamblyn, Bill	Jesu dulcis memoria
Tann, Hilary	Contemplations (21, 22)
	That Jewel-Spirit
	The Moor
Tate, Phyllis	The Gnat
Taylor, Beverly	If I Can Let You Go
Tchaikovsky, Pyotr Ilyich	* The Nutcracker (with Boston Ballet)
Thompson, Randall	Choose something like a star
	The gate of heaven
	Pueri hebraeorum
Tippett, Michael	Crown of the year
Toch, Ernst	La Valse
Tormis, Veljo	Kevadkillud
	Kevadtuul
	Lehtivad pungad
	Öhtune taevas

	Toominga all
	Kollane leek
	Hiliskevad
	Sügismaastikud
Urquhart, Peter	O magnum mysterium
	Hodie Christus natus est
Warlock, Peter	Balulalow
Woll, Erna	*Messe in E*
Wyner, Yehudi	O to be a dragon
Van Ness, Patricia	Epiphany
Vaughan Williams, Ralph	Dirge for Fidele
	God Bless the Master from *Folk Songs*
	Lullaby from *Hodie*
	* Magnificat
	Sigh no more, ladies
	Sweet day
	To the ploughboy (English)
Yannatos, James	The rose
Young, Jennifer	Drink to me only
Yukechev, Yuri	Two Psalm settings from *Gotovo seretse moyo*

Folksongs

Anonymous, Czech	Nas Janycko Nalovany
	Co to mas janicku
Arch, Gwyn	The wind on the moor
Badings, Henk	Les anges dans les campagnes
Barnard, Henk	Africa Medley
	Sivela Kwazulu
	Sila Sila Mili Mili
	Xi Rilela Ngopfu
Bell, Leslie	Ah, Si Mon Moine Voulait Danser
Biggs, John	Il court, le furet
Bingham, Seth	Come all you fair and tender ladies
Brockway, Howard	The nightingale

Davis, K. K.	An unforgotten song (Scottish)
Donovan, Richard	Aye Wauken O! (Scottish)
Dawson, William	Ev'ry time I feel the spirit
Escalada, Oscar	Mudanzas
Estévez, Antonio, arr. J. Carpenter	Mata del Anima Sola
Favero, Alberto, arr. Cangiano	Te quiero
FitzGibbon, Katherine	South African folk song
Fletcher, Percy	Follow Me Down to Carlow
Forbes, Elliot	Three Welsh folk songs
Hamilton, David	I know moon rise
Hillerud, Jan-Åke	Koivisto-polska
Johnson, Hall, adapt. Taylor	Ain't got time to die
Karngard, Bengt	Dagsmeja
Koponen, Glenn	Revivalist Song
Krone, adap. Taylor	Ride the Chariot
Marvin, Jameson	* Ca' the Yowes (Welsh)
	* He's gone away
	Lonesome Road
	Long time ago (English Ballad)
	* Sweet Phoebe (English)
	Voi di vo (Georgian)
	* Wayfarin' Stranger
Masliah, Leo	Biromes y serviltelas (Uruguayan)
Merkù, Pavle	Zeleni polog
Noble, Clifton J.	Deep River
Nordqvist, Gustav	Jul, jul, strålande jul (Swedish Carol)
	Ogura
	Hotaru Koi (Japanese)
Phillips, John	Mary had a Baby
	Steal Away
Santa Cruz, Domingo	Desde el fondo de mi alma
Scott, Tom	Jenny Jenkins
Thomson, Virgil	My Shepherd Will Supply My Need

Tucker, Scott	Sine Nomine (African)
	Dancing (African)
Villa-Lobos, arr. Cabero/Tucker	Estrella é lua nova
Villa-Lobos, Heitor	Canção de Saudade